Science Technology Engineering Math

STEM QUEST

FANTASTIC FORCES
AND
INCREDIBLE MACHINES

BARRON'S

First edition for the United States and Canada
published in 2018 by
Barron's Educational Series, Inc.

Text, design, and illustrations copyright
© Carlton Books Limited 2018,
an imprint of the Carlton Publishing Group,
20 Mortimer Street, London, WIT 3JW

All inquiries should be addressed to:
Barron's Educational Series, Inc.
250 Wireless Boulevard
Hauppauge, NY 11788
www.barronseduc.com

Executive editor: Selina Wood
Managing art editor: Dani Lurie
Design: Claire Barber
Illustrator: Annika Brandow
Picture research: Steve Behan
Production: Yael Steinitz
Editorial consultant: Jack Challoner

ISBN: 978-1-4380-1134-9
Library of Congress Control Number: 2017959665

Date of Manufacture: May 2018
Printed by Oriental Press, Jebel Ali, Dubai, U.A.E.
9 8 7 6 5 4 3 2 1

AUTHOR
Nick Arnold

Nick Arnold is the author of many science books for children, including a best-selling series of yucky but entertaining science facts. When he is not writing, Nick spends his time giving talks to children in bookshops, schools, and libraries.

STEM EDITORIAL CONSULTANT
Georgette Yakman

Georgette Yakman is the founding researcher and creator of the integrative STEAM framework with degrees in Integrated STEM Education, Technology and Fashion Design. She is the CEO of STEAM Education and works in over 20 countries offering educational professional development courses and consulting as an international policy advisor.

ILLUSTRATOR
Kristyna Baczynski

Kristyna Baczynski is an Eisner-nominated comics creator and illustrator. Her work has appeared globally in a myriad of contexts, including magazines, books, clothing, and curtains. If not an illustrator, she would have been a biochemist, so STEM is a subject close to her heart.

The publishers would like to thank the following sources for their kind permission to reproduce the pictures in the book.

9. National Maritime Museum, Greenwich, 11. Public Domain, 17. Bachrach/Getty Images, 25. Hulton Archive/Getty Images, 27. Bettman/Getty Images, 39. Keystone-France/Gamma-Keystone via Getty Images, 41. © Mercedez-Benz, 49. and 51. Public Domain, 53. Hulton Archive/Getty Images, 57. Courtesy of Lehigh University, 60. Universal History Archive/UIG via Getty Images, 63. SSPL/Getty Images, 71. Cynthia Johnson/The LIFE Images Collection/Getty Images, 75. NASA

Every effort has been made to acknowledge correctly and contact the source and/or copyright holder of each picture, and Carlton Books apologizes for any unintentional errors or omissions, which will be corrected in future editions of this book.

Adult supervision is recommended for all activities.

Science Technology Engineering Math

STEM QUEST

FANTASTIC FORCES

AND

INCREDIBLE MACHINES

Nick Arnold

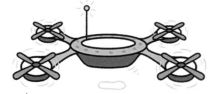

BARRON'S

CONTENTS

WELCOME TO STEM QUEST!

We're the **STEM Squad**, and we'd like to introduce you to the wonderful world of STEM: **Science, Technology, Engineering,** and **Math.** The **STEM Quest** series has a book on each of these fascinating subjects, and we are here to guide you through them. STEM learning gives you real-life examples and experiments to help you relate these subjects to the world around you. We hope you will discover that no matter who you are, you can be whatever you want to be: a scientist, an engineer, a technologist, or a mathematician. Let's take a closer look...

SCIENCE

In science you investigate the world around you.

Carlos and Ella

Super scientist **Carlos** is an expert on supernovas, gravity, and bacteria. **Ella** is Carlos's lab assistant. Carlos is planning a trip to the Amazon rain forest where Ella can collect, organize, and store data!

TECHNOLOGY

In technology you develop products and gadgets to improve our world.

Lewis and Violet

Top techy **Lewis** dreams of being on the first spaceship to Mars. Gadget genius **Violet** was built by Lewis from recycled trash.

ENGINEERING

In engineering you solve problems to create extraordinary structures and machines.

Olive and Clark

Olive is an Incredible engineer who built her first skyscraper (out of dog biscuits) at the age of three. **Clark** was discovered by Olive on a trip to the pyramids of Giza.

MATH

In math you explore numbers, measurements, and shapes.

Sophie and Pierre

Math wizard **Sophie** impressed her class by working out the ratio of popcorn-lovers to doughnut-munchers. **Pierre** is Sophie's computer backup. His computer skills are helping to unlock the mystery of prime numbers.

ENGINEERING IS ABOUT INVESTIGATING AND PLANNING TO CREATE IMPROVED PRODUCTS AND SYSTEMS

Say "engineering" and what pops into your head? Maybe you'll think of forces and machines and construction sites. You'll find plenty of forces and machines in this book, but you'll also find people—the engineers who use science and math to measure forces and examine materials so that they can create wonderful new products and systems. Engineering can be divided into different categories:

SUSTAINABILITY ENGINEERING

BIO / MED / AG / CHEM

MATERIALS & PROCESSES

SYSTEMS & MECHANICS

STRUCTURES

CIVIL
Public spaces, including town and road development.

ENVIRONMENTAL
Sustainability of ecosystems.

OCEAN
Systems in the world's waters.

FLUID
Mechanics and forces of fluids (liquids, gases, and **plasmas**) and the forces that act on them.

BIOTECHNOLOGY
Using parts of living things to create new products.

AGRICULTURE
Farming to grow crops and raise livestock.

BIOCHEMICAL
Chemical processes of living things.

CHEMICAL
Substances that make up **matter.**

BIOMEDICAL
Interacting with living things to improve bodies.

MATERIALS
New materials (mostly solids).

MINING
Extracting minerals from planets.

NUCLEAR
Breakdown (fission) and combining (fusion) of the **nuclei** of **atoms.**

INDUSTRIAL
Evaluating and ordering processes for manufacturing (factories).

MECHANICAL
Parts and machines.

ELECTRICAL
Technology of electricity, components, devices, and systems.

COMPUTING
Developing hardware, software, and networks.

AEROSPACE
Aircraft and spacecraft—aeronautical (in our **atmosphere**) and astronautical (out of our atmosphere).

ARCHITECTURAL
Planning and building construction.

NAVAL ARCHITECTURAL
Maintenance and operation of marine vessels and structures.

Every person needs engineering. We need buildings that are sturdy and pumps and pipes to water our food and heat our homes. We have cars and trains that take us to school and work. We have submersibles that explore the ocean and rockets that take us into space. We have life-saving medicine engineered from tiny microbes.

Our lives are better because of engineering in all of these fields. Which type of engineering interests you the most? Read about them in this book, and one day you might be a problem-solver or master of one of these amazing advancements!

Dream big, and good luck!

MASS MATTERS

Can you feel the force, engineers? Forces and the energy that powers them affect every engineering project in this book—and there are forces acting on your body right now. Take gravity, for example...

gravity pulls objects toward Earth's center

what's the BIG idea?

FORCE OF GRAVITY

Gravity is a force that pulls objects with mass toward each other. Mass is all the matter that makes up something. Objects with a lot of mass—like the earth—have a stronger gravitational pull than objects with less mass. It's gravity that makes objects fall down toward Earth and that makes Earth orbit the sun.

TRY THIS AT HOME

GRAVITY SPEED TEST

What we call "weight" is actually the force of gravity pulling on the mass of an object. If gravity pulls more on heavier objects, they fall faster—right? Let's find out...

YOU WILL NEED:

- ✔ A large ball, such as a soccer ball or basketball
- ✔ A small ball, such as a tennis ball or golf ball
- ✔ A piece of paper
- ✔ A staircase

1. You're going to drop the large ball and the small ball from the same height at the same time. Before you do, make a prediction as to which one will hit the ground first.

2. Drop the balls to see if you made the correct prediction.

3. What about if you dropped one of the balls at the same time as the piece of paper? Will the paper or ball hit the ground first?

4. Drop a ball and the paper to find out.

HOW DOES IT WORK?

The objects fall at the same time! This is because gravity makes all falling objects accelerate (or speed up) at the same rate. Gravity does pull more on heavier things, but this is canceled out because something heavy resists movement more than something light. If you try dropping something light, like paper, what happens? It takes longer to fall because it's slowed down by the air.

TRY THIS AT HOME

RUBBER BAND ENERGY RACES

Along with forces, engineers need to harness **energy**. Energy makes things happen. Let's take a look...

YOU WILL NEED:

- ✔ A rubber band
- ✔ A ruler

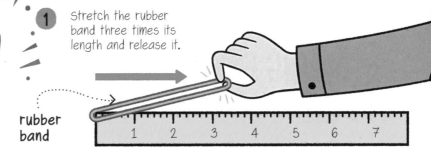

1 Stretch the rubber band three times its length and release it.

rubber band

2 Now stretch the band six times its length and release it.

HOW DOES IT WORK?

When you stretch a rubber band, it gains **potential energy**— an energy stored in the band. When you release it, potential energy changes into **kinetic** (or movement) **energy**. The farther you stretch the band the more energy you store, and the farther the rubber band will fly. You can find out more about potential energy on p. 32.

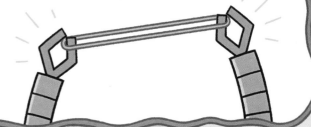

WHO WAS GALILEO?

Italian scientist Galileo Galilei (1564—1642) found that objects of different weight fall at the same speed. He also discovered the science behind **pendulums**—he realized that as a pendulum swings, potential energy turns into kinetic energy as gravity forces the pendulum down. This happens over and over again as the pendulum swings.

ON THE MOVE

There are forces other than gravity and energy that push and pull on objects and influence how things move. Let's check them out, engineers. Time to get moving!

TRY THIS AT HOME

STOPPING AND STARTING

First, let's try out an experiment to find out how things move—or perhaps why they don't move!

YOU WILL NEED:

- ✔ A toy car
- ✔ Corrugated cardboard
- ✔ Scissors
- ✔ Glue
- ✔ A ruler
- ✔ A tape measure
- ✔ A rubber band
- ✔ Two 6 in (15 cm) dowels
- ✔ Aluminum foil
- ✔ A pencil
- ✔ Paper
- ✔ Plastic wrap
- ✔ Water in a spray bottle

1 Cut out four to five pieces of cardboard at least 5 x 10 in (12 x 25 cm) and glue them together. Let them dry.

glue

2 Measure half way down the length of the glued together cardboard and mark a spot with a pencil. Then mark two spots ¾ in (1.5 cm) in from the side of the cardboard. They should be 2½ in (6.5 cm) on either side of the center line. In the two spots, pierce a hole slightly smaller than the dowels with the scissors.

3 Push the two dowels into these holes. Put the rubber band around the dowels. If the dowels are unsteady, add more layers of cardboard.

dowel

holes

4 Put a ruler flat between the dowels, and place the car in front of the rubber band.

ruler

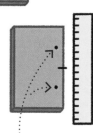

5 On a flat level floor, lay out an area for a track that's at least 4–5 ft (1–1.2-m) track. Place a tape measure along the edge of the track area.

rubber band

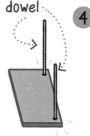

cardboard

6 Cut out three pieces of cardboard about 10 x 36 in (25 x 90 cm).

7 Leave one of the pieces of cardboard as it is, cover the second with aluminum foil, and the third with plastic wrap.

8 Now test the tracks. Pull back the car in the rubber band and let it go. Try each track 3 times, each with different pull-back measurements.

9 Record the distance each time. Can you calculate the **average** of the three distances on each type of surface? Which surfaces have the highest and lowest averages? Which surfaces require more force to travel on them?

10 Now spray water on the tracks, and try the experiment again. Write down your results.

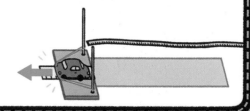

HOW DOES IT WORK?

Before you start, the toy car isn't going anywhere—an object stays still until a force is applied to it. This principle is called **inertia**. When you pushed the car forward, you applied a force to it. The force made the car accelerate. Eventually, the car stopped due to **friction**—the rubbing force between its wheels and the floor. Did you notice a big difference when you covered the track with foil or plastic wrap or water? On which surface did the car travel the farthest? Why do you think this is?

WHO WAS NEWTON?

The English **physicist** Sir Isaac Newton (1643–1727) discovered the **Laws of Motion**. Newton's First Law of Motion explains that objects only move when a force is applied. They then move in a straight line. The greater the mass of an object, the more inertia it has and the harder it is to move.

TRY THIS AT HOME

GETTING IN A SPIN

From cars to computers, many machines depend on spinning or turning. But what are the forces involved?

YOU WILL NEED:

- ✔ An old CD
- ✔ A pen
- ✔ Modeling clay
- ✔ Tape
- ✔ String
- ✔ Scissors
- ✔ Ruler with metric and imperial measurements

1 Push the pen through the central hole of the CD. You may need to add some modeling clay to make it fit snuggly.

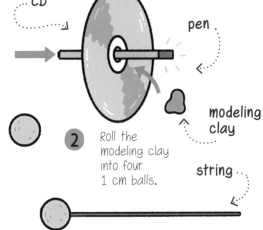

CD

pen

modeling clay

string

2 Roll the modeling clay into four 1 cm balls.

1 cm

3 Mold each ball around a 2½ in (7 cm) piece of string, so you have four balls on four strings.

2½ in (7 cm)

4 Tape the other end of the string pieces to the CD. Try to space them equally apart.

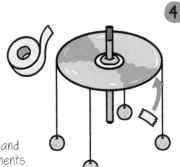

5 Place the end of the pen on a flat surface, and twirl it between your hands.

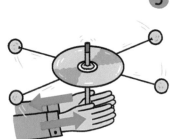

HOW DOES IT WORK?

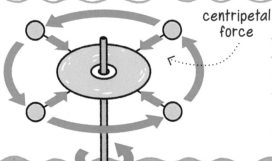

centripetal force

The balls fly out to the side. Your hands create a turning force called **torque** on the pen. The inertia of the balls resist this force, and the balls try to move in a straight line. But when objects move in a circle, another force, known as **centripetal force**, constantly pulls the objects toward the center, stopping them from flying off in a straight line. This centripetal force is produced by the tension in the strings.

BZZZZ! ELECTRICITY!

There's more to engineering than brute force. To power our machines, engineers often use a shocking force we know as electricity. Electricity occurs in the natural world but can be generated to power all sorts of things.

→ what's the BIG idea?

WHAT IS ELECTRICITY?

Everything in the world is made up of tiny building blocks called atoms. In the center of each atom is a **nucleus** with tiny **charged** particles called **protons** and **neutrons**. Whizzing around the nucleus are other particles called **electrons**. Electrons are normally stuck in orbit around the nucleus of atoms. However, in some materials they come loose and move from one atom to another. This flow of "free" electrons is what creates electric **current**.

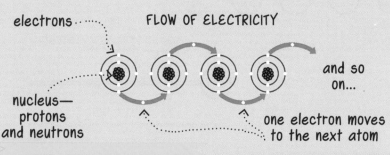

electrons

FLOW OF ELECTRICITY

and so on...

nucleus—protons and neutrons

one electron moves to the next atom

WHAT'S GOING ON?

STATIC ELECTRICITY

Protons in an atom carry a positive electric charge, whereas electrons carry a negative charge. Neutrons have no charge. Inside ordinary atoms there are the same number of protons and electrons, so the charges cancel each other out. However, sometimes when objects touch, electrons can hop between them, causing them to build up a positive or negative charge. This is known as a static charge, or static electricity.

TRY THIS AT HOME

→ THE GHOSTLY CAN

The force of electricity has some tricks up its sleeve, too. Let's investigate.

YOU WILL NEED:

- ✔ A balloon
- ✔ An empty soda can (it must be metal/aluminum)
- ✔ Your hair (it should be clean and dry)
- ✔ A table

1. Inflate the balloon, and knot the neck.

2. Rub the balloon on your hair at least ten times.

3. Hold the balloon close to the can, and place them on the table.

HOW DOES IT WORK?

The can rolls toward the balloon. When you rub the balloon on your hair, electrons move from the hair and build up on the balloon's surface, which becomes negatively charged. The negatively charged electrons attract the positively charged protons in the can, and the can rolls toward the balloon.

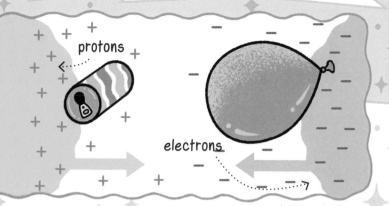

protons

electrons

SUPERHERO PAPER CLIPS

Here's a chance to turn paper clips into superheroes or alien spaceships by making them float in midair.

YOU WILL NEED:

- ✔ A piece of wood
- ✔ Books or small boxes
- ✔ A metal paper clip
- ✔ Adhesive putty
- ✔ A magnet
- ✔ Thread
- ✔ Tape
- ✔ Scissors
- ✔ A ruler with imperial and metric measurements

1 Pile up the books to make two columns on a table. Lay the wood across them. Stick the magnet to the bottom of the wood with the adhesive putty.

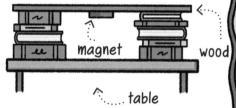

magnet

wood

table

2 Measure the distance between the wood and the tabletop. Cut a length of thread 1 cm shorter than this distance.

2/5 in (1 cm)

3 Tape the paper clip to the thread, and then tape the other end of the thread to the table. Lift the thread up toward the magnet. Watch what happens.

paper clip

tape

thread

HOW DOES IT WORK?

magnetic force

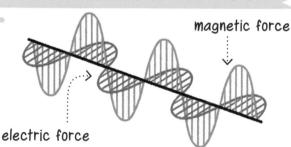

electric force

The paper clip floats in midair because it's attracted to the magnet. The magnetic force is actually created by electrons in the atoms. All charged particles (protons and electrons) are affected by electric and magnetic forces. These two forces combine to produce **electromagnetic waves** (above)—and light is one example of an electromagnetic wave.

IN FACT...

filament

LET THERE BE LIGHT

Electricity can also travel as a flow of electric charge, known as electric current. It can flow from a battery or a main power supply to your home. Electricity can be transformed into other types of energy. For instance, an electric lightbulb converts electrical energy to heat and light by heating a wire called a filament so that it glows white hot.

MATERIAL WORLD

Engineers need to think about which material is best for a job. Does it need to be strong, flexible, or waterproof? There are thousands of materials to choose from. Some are natural, but many are synthetic (made by people).

what's the BIG idea?

ALL ABOUT MATERIALS

Many of the materials that engineers use fall into these four categories:

1. Metals are natural materials extracted from the ground. Most are solid, with a gray or silver appearance. Many metals are tough, hard, and strong and are good conductors—they let electricity pass through them easily.

2. Ceramics are made by heating clay (fine particles of rock or earth) in an oven called a kiln. Pots are made of ceramics. Glass is a ceramic material. Ceramics are insulators—they do not let electricity pass through them easily.

3. Polymers are materials made from long strings of **molecules** (atoms joined together). Polymers can be found in nature, such as wood and rubber. They can also be made by humans from natural things—for instance, plastic is made from oil.

4. Composites are made of combinations of at least two or three metals, polymers, and ceramics. They can be tough but flexible and are used in many things, from window sills to sports equipment.

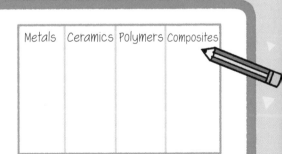

TRY THIS AT HOME

MATERIAL SCAVENGER HUNT

YOU WILL NEED:

- ✔ An adult helper
- ✔ A pencil
- ✔ A piece of paper

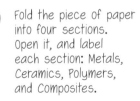

1 Fold the piece of paper into four sections. Open it, and label each section: Metals, Ceramics, Polymers, and Composites.

Metals	Ceramics	Polymers	Composites

2 Look around your house or ask an adult to take you around your neighborhood to search for things that are made of each type of material. Write them down in the appropriate section on your piece of paper.

3 Now turn the paper over and list things you could make with each of the materials.

4 Think about what you could do to each of the materials to change them. For instance, how could you make metal more flexible?

5 Now see if you can come up with your own invention made out of one or more of the materials.

TRY THIS AT HOME

NOT-SO-DRASTIC PLASTIC

We've seen that ceramics, plastics, and composites are made by people. Here's how to make your very own plastic.

YOU WILL NEED:

- ✔ An adult helper
- ✔ Whole milk (not skim)
- ✔ A measuring cup
- ✔ Vinegar
- ✔ A teaspoon
- ✔ A pot
- ✔ A bowl
- ✔ A fine strainer
- ✔ A stove or hot plate
- ✔ A wooden spoon

1 Ask an adult to help you heat 5 fl oz (150 ml) of milk until it simmers.

2 Add 4 teaspoons of vinegar.

vinegar

3 Stir until clumps fully form, and then remove the pot from the heat.

4 Pour the mixture through the strainer into the bowl.

5 Carefully pour off the remaining liquid, and squish together the solids with the teaspoon.

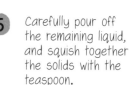

You could even make some simple rubbery sculptures!

WARNING! BEWARE, HEAT!

HOW DOES IT WORK?

Congratulations! You've made a rubbery plastic! Like all plastics, it's made up of long stringy molecules. In this case, the molecules are a type of **protein** called casein. The **acid** in the vinegar separates the protein and fat in the milk.

fat

protein

BIGGER, BETTER BUILDINGS

Engineering isn't just about making machines. It's also about designing and making improvements to structures, such as houses, skyscrapers, and bridges. That's what's known as architectural engineering. Grab your hard hats, engineers—let's investigate!

FEEL THE FORCE

There are many forces and stresses on a building, including the force of gravity. Different shapes distribute weight and handle pressure from forces differently. Let's make some 3-D framed house shapes to see where they **bow** and flex under pressure.

YOU WILL NEED:

☑ Straws or pipe cleaners
☑ Scissors
☑ A ruler
☑ A pen
☑ Tape

1 Think about whether you'd like to make a square frame, a pyramid frame, or a frame with many sides.

× 12

2 For a square frame, you will need 12 straws or pipe cleaners all of the same length. Use a ruler to mark equal sections on a pipe cleaner or straw, and then cut them.

3 Stick the pieces together, as shown, with tape.

4 You will need 6 equal lengths of pipe cleaner or straw to make a pyramid frame.

5 Here's another example, but you can make any shape you like.

6 Why not build a tall tower?

7 Press down on the shapes with your hand to see which shapes seem stronger. Try twisting them, too.

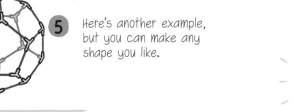

HOW DOES IT WORK?

This activity helps you test the effects of force (pressure) and torque (twist) on the different frames. Which frame was the most stable? Which frame was the most unstable? Try adding some extra pieces of straw for more support. You could add pieces to the corners. What difference does that make?

TALL TALES

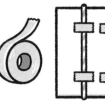
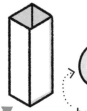

tape

straws

For taller buildings, you need lighter but stronger structures. In real life, skyscrapers have to resist gravity and the horizontal force of strong winds.

1 Fold the cardstock in half, and then fold each half in half again to make a rectangular shape.

2 Open the cardstock and tape the straws to it as shown above.

YOU WILL NEED:

☑ A rectangular piece of cardstock

☑ Four toothpicks

☑ Four straws

☑ A piece of polystyrene

☑ Tape

3 Refold the cardstock and secure the sides with tape. Place the toothpicks in the polystyrene and push the cardstock model down so that the straws fit over the toothpicks.

toothpicks

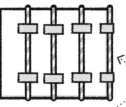

HOW DOES IT WORK?

Congratulations! You've built a light but strong skyscraper model. You've created strong outer walls by reinforcing them with straws in each corner of the model. The toothpicks placed in the polystyrene provide a sturdy **foundation**.

IN FACT...

SKYSCRAPERS

In real skyscrapers, rigid steel frames provide strength (but are lighter than most solid walls). Attached to the steel frame are usually glass panels, which form walls. For extra strength, there are columns inside or on the outside walls. Skyscrapers also have foundations that go deep into the ground to make them more secure.

WHO WAS FULLER?

Buckminster Fuller (1895–1983) was an American architect and inventor who is famous for his work on the geodesic domes. These are dome shapes that have extra triangular-shaped supports that make the dome even stronger.

17

SUPPORTING STRUCTURES

Engineers, we have a problem! A big building with a heavy roof pushes out your walls. But columns, arches, and domes can make your building stronger and lighter—and buttresses can hold it up. What's their secret?

4. dome

1. columns

2. arch

3. buttress

what's the BIG idea?

BUILDING INSPECTION

Let's look at the parts of a building in more detail:

1. Columns support a roof.
2. The weight of a roof pushes down and around an arch. It also pushes sideways so the sides of the arch need support from a wall or buttress.
3. A buttress stops sideways movement of a wall or arch.
4. A dome is like a three-dimensional arch. The downward force runs over the dome, but there are sideways forces near its base. Many domes have rings or chains around them to stop this.

TRY THIS AT HOME

LIVING ARCHES

It's easy to check out the forces on arches and buttresses. All you need is a little help from your friends.

YOU WILL NEED:

- ✔ Two friends
- ✔ An open space with a soft floor
- ✔ Measuring tape

1 With a friend, put out your hands and lean toward each other so that you support each other on the palms of your hands.

2 Note how far apart you can stand and still be supported. Ask your second friend to measure how far apart you are standing.

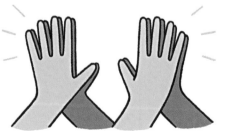

3 Ask your second friend to push you—gently! You can all swap places and compare your experiences.

4 Stand in front of two large objects or walls, roughly the same distance apart as you were standing. Repeat step 1.

HOW DOES IT WORK?

When you tried step 1, did you feel forces pushing on your hands and pushing you apart? When you stood against a wall, was it easier? Just like a real arch, your human arch is much stronger if its sides are supported. This is where buttresses come in handy.

A WEIGHTY MATTER

What about columns and domes—why do we need them? Let's find out.

YOU WILL NEED:

- ✔ Three cardboard boxes of different sizes, thicknesses, and shapes
- ✔ Six cardboard tubes
- ✔ Three plastic bowls of different sizes, thicknesses, and shapes
- ✔ Books
- ✔ A pen and paper

1 Place one cardboard box upside down, and put books on it until it starts to sag at the top.

books

2 Place one bowl upside down, and support it on a circle of cardboard tubes that are standing up. Place the same books on the bowl. What do you notice?

3 Repeat steps 1 and 2 with the other cardboard boxes and bowls, but using the same books each time. When does the structure sag? When does it collapse? Write down your observations.

HOW DOES IT WORK?

The bowl and tubes are lighter, and they will withstand the weight better than the box. The bowl works like a dome and the tubes work like columns. Which structure was the strongest? How did the material, shape, or size of the cardboard boxes and bowls impact your results?

IN FACT...

WONDER DOMES

Look out for domes in some of the world's most famous buildings, such as the Capitol Dome in Washington, D.C., the Florence Cathedral in Italy, or the Taj Mahal in India. They demonstrate some of the most incredible engineering and building design ever seen!

BRIDGES AND TUNNELS

Over the ages, an important job for engineers has been to find a way to cross water, and more recently, roads and railroads. Engineers, let's take a look at these crucial crossings!

TRY THIS AT HOME

BUILD A BRIDGE

Here's how to make and test some bridges of your own.

YOU WILL NEED:

- ✔ Straws or pipe cleaners
- ✔ Two piles of books
- ✔ Pieces of thin cardstock
- ✔ Scissors
- ✔ A pencil
- ✔ A ruler
- ✔ A toy car
- ✔ Tape
- ✔ Weights (small household objects)

1 Decide which of the bridges in the examples below that you would like to build. Cut the straws or pipe cleaners to match the lengths of the beams on the bridges, and tape them together as shown. You can also build a new bridge of your own.

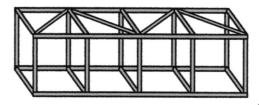
beam bridge

truss bridge

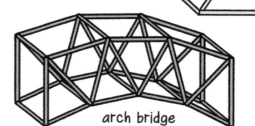
arch bridge

2 Cut a strip of cardstock to fit the length and width of your bridge. This will be the decking or "floor" of your bridge.

3 Now test your bridge. Put it over two piles of books, and push the car across. Tape weights to the car to see at what point your bridge starts to sag, and measure how much it dips.

HOW DOES IT WORK?

Beam bridges are made of horizontal beams with some vertical beams for extra support. Truss bridges are made stronger by triangle supports. Arch bridges use arch structures to push weight outward so that the weight is distributed evenly across the bridge rather than at one point in the middle. How can you strengthen or lighten your bridge to make it stronger or strong enough but less expensive to build?

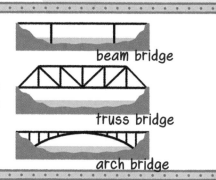

beam bridge

truss bridge

arch bridge

GOING UNDERGROUND

A tunnel has to be really strong—but what's the best shape for a tunnel?

YOU WILL NEED:

- ✔ A cardboard box wider than its height
- ✔ A cardboard tube (the tube needs to be same thickness of cardboard as the box and about the same depth)
- ✔ A shovel or trowel
- ✔ An area of ground where you're allowed to dig a hole
- ✔ A ruler

1 Bury the cardboard box under about 1 in (2.5 cm) of soil. Stand on it.

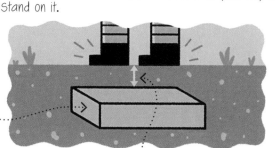

cardboard box

2 Repeat step 1 for the tube.

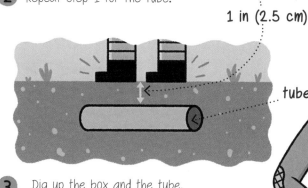

1 in (2.5 cm)

tube

3 Dig up the box and the tube.

HOW DOES IT WORK?

After the experiment, the box is more flattened than the tube. A tube is a strong shape because the downward force is distributed around its sides. Although a box is strong, it's more likely to buckle when a force is applied from above. This is why engineers design tunnels with tubes rather than long boxes. Think of ways you can make the tube stronger to take more pressure or to be able to carry water.

box

tube

RAMP IT UP!

Ready to move on, engineers? It's time to roll up our sleeves and check out some basic parts found in tools and machines. Let's start with incredible ramps and wedges!

TRY THIS AT HOME

A SLIPPERY SLOPE

A ramp may sound basic, but it gives you super powers to lift weights with less effort.

YOU WILL NEED:

- ✔ Books or other items you can pile up
- ✔ String
- ✔ A ball (it needs to be smaller than the box)
- ✔ A cardboard box
- ✔ Wide tape
- ✔ Scissors

1 Wrap the string a few times around the ball and knot it.

2 Pile the books as high as the box sides. Try to drag the ball up the side of the book pile.

3 Turn the box upside down, and cut along the dotted lines as shown.

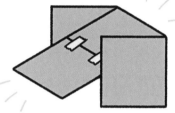

4 Fold out the top and side of the box, and make these sides into a rigid slope using tape on both sides of the slope. You may need to tape another piece of cardboard underneath the seam for support.

5 Place the box against the pile of books and try to drag the ball up the slope.

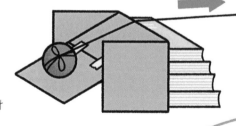

HOW DOES IT WORK?

With the slope, it takes less effort to drag the ball up. The slope is a ramp, and it works like this...

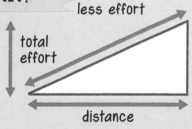

less effort

total effort

distance

A ramp reduces the effort needed to raise a weight by the distance it covers. A longer ramp means more distance to cover but with less effort.

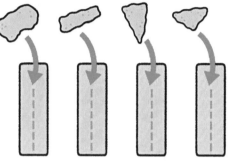

what's the BIG idea?

A wedge is like a ramp on the move. You move an object a distance up a ramp with less effort, and a wedge moves a distance in relation to an object with less effort. Cutting tools, snowplows, and zippers all use wedges to save effort.

TRY THIS AT HOME

DRIVE A WEDGE

In this simple activity you're going to explore the power of the wedge shape!

YOU WILL NEED:

- ✔ Slices of hard cheese and apple

- ✔ Four small stones (about 1–2 in/ 2–3 cm across) of different shapes— rounded, square, and two that are wedge-shaped—narrow at one end and wide at the other. The wedge-shaped stones can be fat or short, thin or long (wash the stones before use)

- ✔ A cutting board

- ✔ A pencil and paper

1 Cut the cheese into "log" shapes and place them on a cutting board.

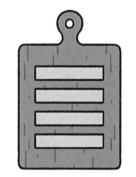

2 Try cutting one of the cheese logs lengthwise with one of the stones. Do the same for three more cheese logs and three different stones.

3 Write down what you discover about how the different stones work when they cut the cheese.

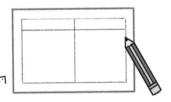

⚠ **WARNING! STONES MAY BE DIRTY. WASH BEFORE USE!**

4 Repeat steps 1 and 2 with the apple pieces.

input force
output force

wedge shape

HOW DOES IT WORK?

You will probably find that the long, thin wedge-shaped stone cuts the cheese and apple pieces the most easily. Using a wedge not only increases the strength of the force but also changes the direction of the force. The force goes outward, making it easier to break the pieces apart. The shallower the wedge angle the more the force is magnified—but the farther you have to push it into the cheese and apple pieces to break them.

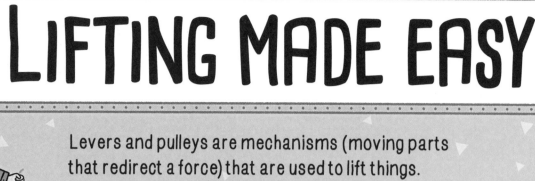

LIFTING MADE EASY

Levers and pulleys are mechanisms (moving parts that redirect a force) that are used to lift things. They are found in many types of machines. What exactly do they do? Let's investigate.

SEESAW SURPRISE

We all love to play on a seesaw, but here's another way you can play with one by experimenting with it as a **lever**!

YOU WILL NEED:

✔ A large binder clip

✔ Scissors

✔ Tape

✔ Two small, light plastic cups

✔ Small coins

✔ A wooden or plastic 12 in (30 cm) ruler

1 Take out the handles from the triangular part of the binder clip by squeezing the two sides of each handle inward. The triangular piece you are left with is now your **fulcrum**.

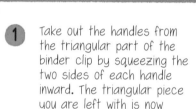

handles

2 Tape the plastic cups to both ends of the ruler. Place the ruler on your fulcrum to complete your lever. Add coins of differing weight to each cup.

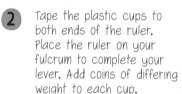

fulcrum ·······>

3 Practice moving coins from one cup to the other. See if you can keep the lever balanced. Slide the ruler from left to right so that the position of the fulcrum under the ruler changes. How does that affect the balance of the seesaw?

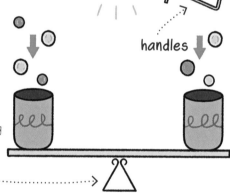

24

HOW DOES IT WORK?

Place other objects other than cups and coins on the lever. Experiment to see how much weight on one side of the lever is needed to lift the other side with different objects. You can also try moving the fulcrum to different positions, too. You'll find that the closer the weight is to the fulcrum, the less effort is needed on the other side of the lever to lift the weight.

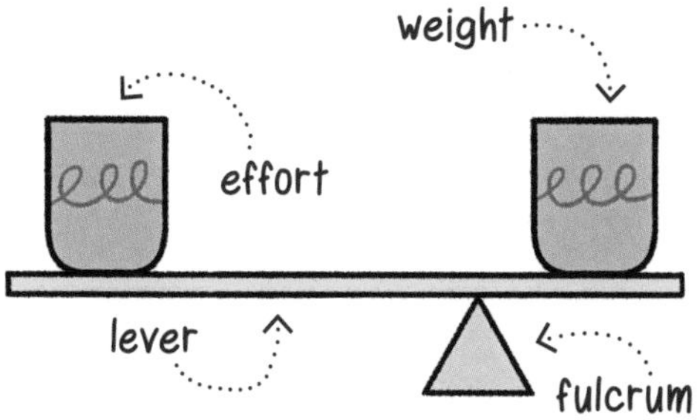

weight

effort

lever   fulcrum

IN FACT...

HOW DO PULLEYS WORK?

Pulleys are simple mechanisms that people have used throughout history to help lift loads with less effort.

A pulley is a wheel with a rope around it. By pulling down on the rope, you can lift a load. When you combine two pulleys, you can lift an object more easily, with much less effort, because the load is shared by two ropes, as shown—but you have to pull the rope twice the distance.

You'll find pulley mechanisms in machines, such as cranes, escalators, and elevators.

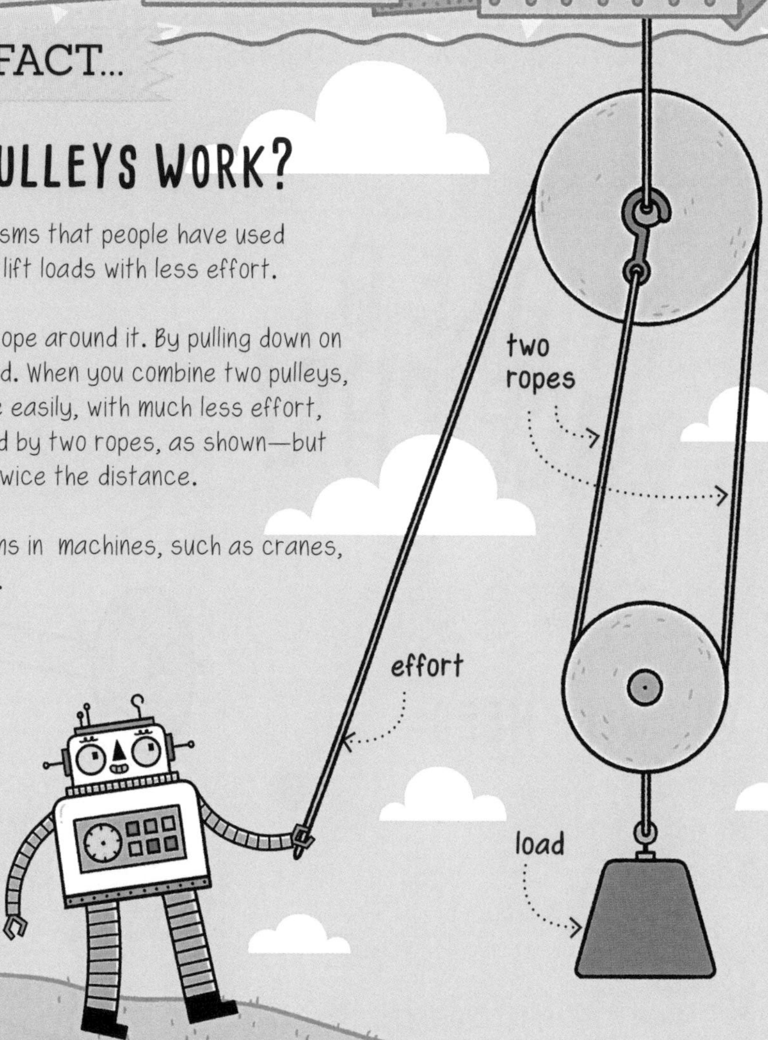

two ropes

effort

load

WHO WAS ARCHIMEDES?

Ancient Greek mathematician and scientist Archimedes (287 B.C.E.–212 B.C.E.) was one of the first people to investigate and explain how levers work.

THE WHEEL DEAL

Guess what? Wheels are machines, too! Wheels aren't just for cars or roller blades, they are incredible mechanisms used in many different machines. Roll on, engineers!

TRY THIS AT HOME

MAKE A RACE CAR!

OK—it's not a real race car but once you see it move, who cares?

YOU WILL NEED:

- ✔ An adult helper
- ✔ Two clothespins
- ✔ Four identical buttons, about 1 in (2.5 cm) in diameter
- ✔ A straw
- ✔ Two paper clips or thin copper wire
- ✔ Scissors
- ✔ Glue or tape
- ✔ A large piece of cardboard
- ✔ Books
- ✔ A pen and paper

WARNING! SHARP PAPER CLIP EDGES

1 Cut two 1¼ in (3 cm) lengths of straw. With adult help, straighten the paper clips with the pliers, and thread one through each straw. The paper clips need to be free to move in the straws.

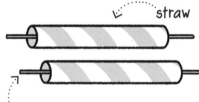

straw

paper clip

2 Attach each paper clip to two buttons. Depending on the type of button, wrap the paper clip through its central holes or through the loop at the back. The buttons are your wheels. The wheels shouldn't touch the ends of the straws.

button

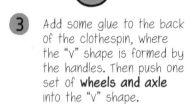

3 Add some glue to the back of the clothespin, where the "V" shape is formed by the handles. Then push one set of **wheels and axle** into the "V" shape.

4 Add some glue in the gap at the other end of the clothespin. Place the other wheel and axle in the gap. If it's loose, secure it with tape.

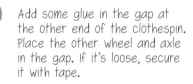

glue

VROOM!

5 Prop the cardboard on a pile of books. First, try pushing the clothespin without the wheels down the slope. Now let your car run down the slope. Write down your results. You could make another car and have a race!

HOW DOES IT WORK?

The car wheels turn because the stretched out paper clips are free to rotate separately from the body of the car. All wheels and axles work like this. You'll probably find that the clothespin with the wheels rolls down the slope faster than the one without wheels. That's because there is less friction between the straw and the paper clip than there is between the clothespin and the cardboard. Try covering the wheels with aluminum foil, plastic wrap, and paper, and time how long the car takes to roll down the slope each time. Write down your results.

what's the BIG idea?

The two parts of a wheel and axle are connected so that they always turn together. The rim of the wheel turns faster and farther than the axle—so if you turn the wheel, you can apply great force to the axle, but if you turn the axle, you can make the wheel turn much faster.

In some inventions, this effect is used the opposite way. For example, when a driver turns the steering wheel of a car, the wheel moves a greater distance than the axle, but the axle turns with greater effort. This helps the driver turn the wheels more easily.

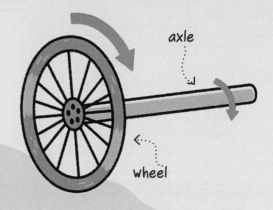

axle

wheel

WHO WAS DUNLOP?

John Dunlop (1840–1921) was a Scottish inventor and veterinarian who made the first practical pneumatic (blow-up) tire that we now see everywhere on cars, trucks, and bicycles.

GRINDING GEARS

Gears are sets of wheels with teeth (notches) on them that interlock when they turn. They look simple, but these wondrous wheels are a key part of many complex machines.

what's the BIG idea?

INCREDIBLE GEARS

Gears increase the force or speed of moving parts. When a gear turns, it transfers its force to a second gear that turns in the opposite direction. If one wheel drives another with fewer teeth, the wheel with fewer teeth turns with less force but faster. If a wheel drives another that has more teeth, the wheel with more teeth turns more slowly but with greater force than the other.

Which way will this turn?

TRY THIS AT HOME

GET IN GEAR

The gears on a bicycle help you reach the speed you want. Have you ever wondered how they let you pedal uphill more easily?

YOU WILL NEED:

- ✔ A bicycle with gears
- ✔ A friend

1 Ask a friend to help you turn the bike upside down, and then click the bike into low gear. Turn the pedals until the chain clicks onto the large gear cog. Turn the pedals again, and watch how the large gear cog turns.

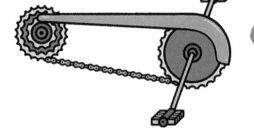

2 Click into high gear—the chain should move to the small cog. Turn the pedals and watch how the small gear cog turns.

HOW DOES IT WORK?

The large gear cog turns more slowly, but with more force than the small gear wheel. Top gear (a small gear cog) is ideal for building up speed over flat ground. Low gear (a large gear cog) allows you to pedal uphill with less effort.

AN UNEXPECTED TURN

Now's your chance to experiment with some homemade gears!

YOU WILL NEED:

- ✔ An adult helper
- ✔ Two pieces of corrugated cardboard
- ✔ A pen
- ✔ A sheet of tracing paper
- ✔ Scissors
- ✔ Two push pins
- ✔ Tape

⚠ WARNING! SHARP PIN!

1 Take the tracing paper, and trace the two gear wheels below (A and B).

2 Cut the gears out, and tape them to the piece of cardboard.

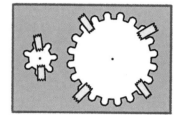

3 Cut around the traced shapes so you are left with two cardboard gear shapes.

4 Place the gears on the second piece of cardboard with their teeth interlocking. Ask an adult to help you push the map pins through the centers of each wheel.

5 Turn the small wheel and watch how the large wheel turns. Now turn the large wheel and watch how the small wheel turns.

A
(20 teeth)

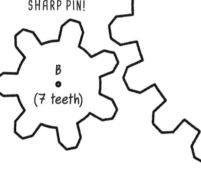

B
(7 teeth)

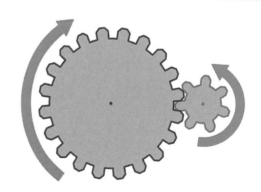

HOW DOES IT WORK?

You'll see that your gear wheels not only turn in opposite directions—they turn at different speeds, too. When the large gear wheel turns once, the small gear wheel turns 2.86 times (20 teeth = 2.86 x 7 teeth). The small wheel turns 2.86 times quicker but with less force than the large wheel, and 2.86 turns of the small wheel gives the same force as one full turn of the large wheel. This is called the gear ratio of the difference in the gears. When gears are connected to other parts of machines, for instance, in a car or bike, they help control the force and speed at which the machines move.

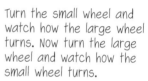

RACKS, RATCHETS, CAMS & CRANKS

Gears are great, but engineers know that there are other simple mechanisms that also help to make machines work. Let's take a closer look! Can you figure out what they do?

HOW DO RACKS, CAMS, AND CRANKS WORK?

Like all mechanisms, racks, cams, and cranks change the direction of a force.

crank arm · crank wheel

crank arm · crank wheel

rod · rod

cam

cam

pinion

rack

2. The crank and rod turn the rotary (turning) movement of the crank wheel into side-to-side motion of the crank arm. Also, if you move the arm from side-to-side, the wheel turns around.

3. As the cam turns around, it forces the rod up. When gravity makes the rod fall, the cam pushes it up again.

1. A pinion is a gear wheel. Its teeth interlock with the rack teeth and its turning motion is turned into motion in a line.

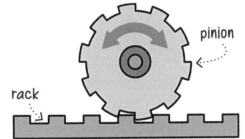

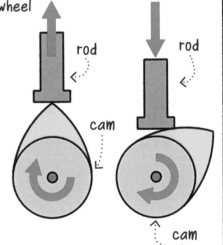

HOW DOES A RATCHET WORK?

The ratchet is different. Could you make one yourself and check out what it does?

YOU WILL NEED:

- ✔ An adult helper
- ✔ A piece of cardstock
- ✔ A pencil
- ✔ Scissors
- ✔ A foam plate
- ✔ Thick cardstock
- ✔ A sheet of corkboard (or glue cardboard sheets in layers until they're thicker than a push pin's point)
- ✔ Two push pins
- ✔ A ruler with metric and imperial measurements

⚠️ **WARNING! SHARP PIN!**

1 Draw a circle about 3 in (8 cm) across on cardstock.

3 in (8 cm)

2 Within this circle, draw a second circle 1 cm smaller all the way around.

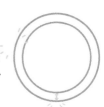
1 cm

3 Draw ratchet wheel teeth between the two lines as shown. Try to make the ratchet teeth the same size and evenly spaced around the circle.

4 Cut out the ratchet wheel, place it on the plate, and draw around it.

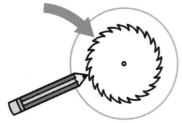

5 Cut out the ratchet wheel shape from the plate.

6 With adult help, insert a push pin into the center of the ratchet wheel, and pin it to the corkboard.

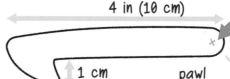
4 in (10 cm)
1 cm   pawl

7 Draw the pawl shape as shown on thick cardstock and cut it out. Insert a push pin through the pawl at the point marked "x" in the drawing. Pin the pawl to the corkboard so that it will engage with the teeth of the ratchet wheel. Turn the ratchet wheel.

HOW DOES IT WORK?

The pawl locks into the teeth on the wheel so that the wheel can only turn in one direction. Try turning the wheel over—does that make a difference? Ratchets control the direction of a turning force so that it only goes one way. You'll find them in many things, from roller blinds to mechanical clocks and seat belt rollers.

pawl
ratchet wheel

STRETCHY AND SPRINGY STUFF

Mechanical engineers need to know all about how energy works. First, let's take a look at stretchy and springy machines. They're powered by potential energy.

what's the BIG idea?

POTENTIAL ENERGY

Remember the rubber band experiment on page 9? Potential energy is stored energy that you can use later. It's stored when you change the position of an object and released when the object returns to its position. Here are two types of potential energy.

The rock stores gravitational potential energy as it's rolled uphill. It releases its energy when it falls.

The spring stores elastic potential energy when it's pushed down. What do you think happens next?

TRY THIS AT HOME

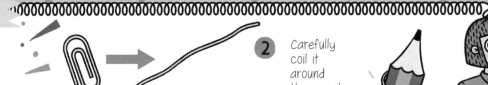

SPRING TIME!

Here's a simple experiment to show how a spring works.

YOU WILL NEED:

- ✔ An adult helper
- ✔ A paper clip
- ✔ A pencil

1 Ask an adult to help you straighten the paper clip into a wire.

2 Carefully coil it around the pencil to make a spring shape.

3 Push the spring down.

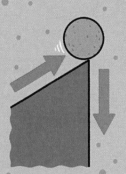

WARNING! PAPER CLIPS CAN BE SHARP

HOW DOES IT WORK?

When you press a spring down, the spring shape stores movement energy as potential energy. It releases energy when it springs back up. No wonder springs are springy!

PLANE POWER!

In this activity you will use elastic potential energy to launch a plane.

YOU WILL NEED:

- ✔ An adult helper
- ✔ A piece of corrugated cardboard
- ✔ Paper or thin cardstock
- ✔ A paper clip
- ✔ Push pins
- ✔ A rubber band
- ✔ A hole punch
- ✔ Tape
- ✔ Books

 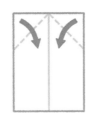 

1 Make the paper plane as shown above.

Fold angled edges into the center line.

Fold down wings on each side along the dotted line, as shown.

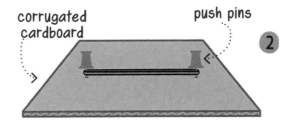

corrugated cardboard

push pins

2 Place the push pins in the corrugated cardboard. They should be the same distance apart as the length of your rubber band. Loop the rubber band over it.

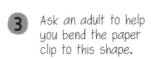

paper clip

3 Ask an adult to help you bend the paper clip to this shape.

hole

tape

4 Use the hole punch to make a hole in the plane nose. Thread the end of the paper clip into it and secure it with tape.

⚠️ WARNING! PAPER CLIPS CAN BE SHARP. NEVER FIRE THE PLANE AT PEOPLE!

potential energy

5 It's time to test your plane launcher. You could prop the corrugated cardboard up on books to make a launch ramp. Hook the paper clip under the rubber band, pull the plane back, and release the plane!

kinetic energy

HOW DOES IT WORK?

When you pull the plane back, you store energy in the rubber band. As you pull a rubber band, its molecules are formed into lines. Let the band go and they snap back, turning potential energy back into kinetic energy, which sets your plane soaring!

before   stretched   after

PUFFING AND CHUGGING

Along with buildings and machines, engineers create vehicles. Let's start with the first strong engines, steam engines! Pull that whistle, and check out what makes a steam engine rumble.

what's the BIG idea?

WHY HAVE POWERED MACHINES?

Muscle power can be slow, and people can only do so much before they get tired! But machines never get tired (although their parts can wear out or break). Machines turn potential energy in fuel (such as coal or oil) to kinetic energy for movement or work.

TRY THIS AT HOME

THE SECRET OF STEAM ENGINES

The secret of **steam** engines is simple. It's all about what happens to air when you heat it and cool it. Are you ready for another experiment?

YOU WILL NEED:

- ✔ An adult helper
- ✔ Two large bowls
- ✔ Two plastic bottles
- ✔ Ice
- ✔ Water
- ✔ A balloon

!

WARNING! ICE CAN BURN AND HOT WATER CAN SCALD!

1 Fill one bowl with ice and cold water.

ice water

2 Blow up the balloon a few times until it's saggy.

3 Attach the balloon to the neck of the bottle.

4 With adult help, fill the second bowl with hot water, and wait a few minutes.

hot water

5 Stand the bottle in the bowl of hot water and watch.

6 Attach the balloon to the second bottle and stand it in the ice and cold water bowl. What happens?

HOW DOES IT WORK?

The balloon partly inflates when it's in the hot water and deflates when it's in the cold water. When the bottle is in the hot water, the air inside warms up. The air molecules have more energy and move faster. They hit the sides of the balloon harder and make the balloon expand. When you place the bottle in cold water, the opposite occurs. The molecules slow down and draw closer together, and the balloon deflates.

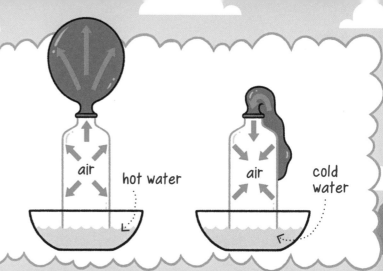

air — hot water

air — cold water

WHAT'S GOING ON?

HOW DOES A STEAM ENGINE WORK?

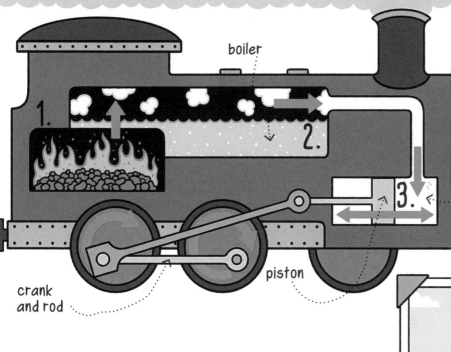

boiler

1.

2.

3.

cylinder

crank and rod

piston

IN FACT...

ON THE BOIL

It's now possible to build supercritical steam boilers. These are so powerful that they can turn water to steam instantly. Imagine a kettle like that!

1. Water is heated and turns to steam in the boiler. The hot steam expands just like the hot air in your experiment.

2. Steam pushes a **piston** to the end of a cylinder. In many **engines**, a second blast of steam from the boiler pushes the piston back.

3. A crank and rod often converts the back and forth movement of the piston into the rotary (turning) movement of a wheel, and the train moves.

IN FACT...

STEAM SHIPS

Steam has also been used to power cars and boats. In a steam boat, the engine is connected to propellers or paddles that drive the boat forward. The first steam ships, or steamers, were in operation in the early 1800s. These boats were less dependent on the wind than boats with sails that came before them.

FLOATING MAGNET TRAINS

Most trains run on rails, but some modern trains hover in midair. Let's check out how this incredible floating technology works, engineers!

RIDE THE RAILS

First, let's see how traditional rails work. Time to make your own train tracks!

YOU WILL NEED:

- ✔ An adult helper
- ✔ Cardstock
- ✔ Two thin wooden dowels
- ✔ Four plastic bottle caps
- ✔ Toothpicks
- ✔ Adhesive putty
- ✔ A ruler
- ✔ Glue
- ✔ Tape
- ✔ Scissors

1 Place the dowels on a flat surface in a **parallel** position. The distance between the dowels should be the length of the toothpicks. Check that they're straight with a ruler, and hold them in place with putty. These are your rails.

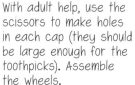

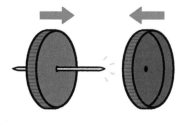

2 With adult help, use the scissors to make holes in each cap (they should be large enough for the toothpicks). Assemble the wheels.

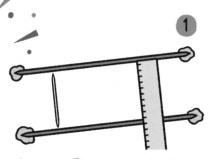

3 Cut circles out of the cardstock, a little larger than the caps, and glue them to the caps. (The rim of the wheels need to be smaller than the depth of the dowels so they will sit on the rails, not the floor).

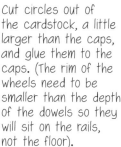

4 Fold a piece of cardstock into a rectangle, and tape it to the toothpicks. This is your train car.

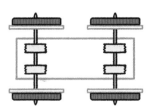

5 Place the train car with the wheels on the rails and push it.

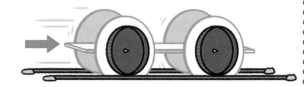

The wheels should fit snuggly along the track. If the wheels start going off course, the cardstock rims push them back on course. Real train wheels have a rim like this, keeping the train on the rails even when the train goes around a bend.

TRY THIS AT HOME

EXPLORING THE MAGLEV

Maglev is short for "magnetic levitation." Levitation means to rise without support. Let's see how maglev trains operate!

YOU WILL NEED:

- ✔ A rectangular piece of cardstock
- ✔ Tape
- ✔ A pencil
- ✔ A ruler
- ✔ Enough bar magnets to stretch the length of the cardstock, with one to spare

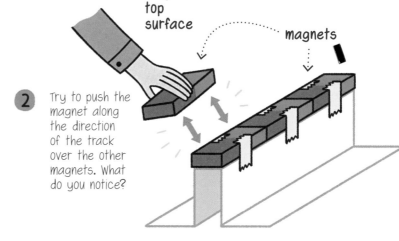

1 Draw lines and fold the cardstock into the shape shown below, making the top surface the same width as your magnets. Tape the magnets onto the top surface, end to end. Hold up the spare magnet above your rail, with its north or south pole above the same poles of the magnet on the end of the rail. The magnets should repel each other.

top surface

magnets

2 Try to push the magnet along the direction of the track over the other magnets. What do you notice?

HOW DOES IT WORK?

The opposite poles of magnets attract but the same poles repel each other, which is why there is a force pushing apart your spare magnet and magnets on the rail. Maglev trains are powered by electromagnets that are produced by an electric current. A magnetic coil in the track repels the large magnets on the train's undercarriage so that it floats above the rail and there's no friction. Maglev trains are much faster and use less energy than trains that run on diesel. They can travel at speeds over 370 mph (600 km/h).

STEP ON THE GAS!

Millions of people drive cars every day. They are powered mostly by gasoline, diesel fuel, or electricity. How do cars work, and what gives them that VROOOM factor?

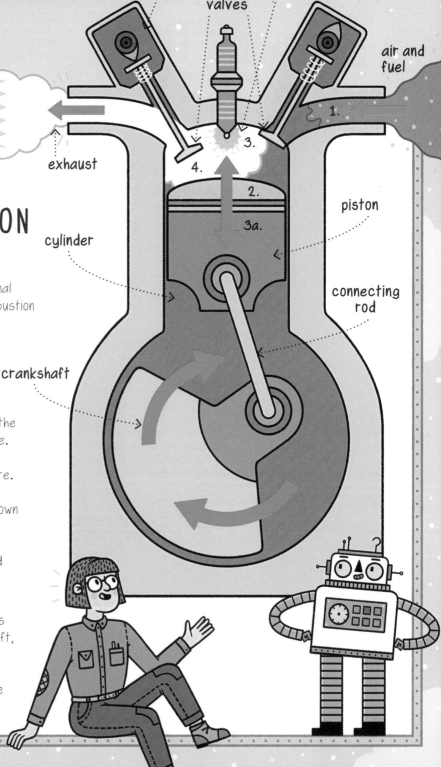

cams

spark ignites

valves

air and fuel

exhaust

cylinder

crankshaft

1.

3.

4.

2.

3a.

piston

connecting rod

what's the BIG idea?

HOW DOES AN INTERNAL COMBUSTION ENGINE WORK?

Most cars are powered by a gasoline-fueled internal combustion engine. It gets its name from the combustion (burning of fuel) that occurs inside the engine. It works on a four-stroke cycle like this:

1. The **piston** moves down. The air and fuel mixture is sucked into the cylinder.

2. The piston moves up, compressing (squashing) the air and fuel—raising its temperature and pressure.

3. An electric spark ignites the air and fuel mixture. This turns potential energy in gasoline into kinetic energy. The burning gas forces the piston back down (3a). This is sometimes called the power stroke.

4. The piston rises again, and waste gas is forced out of the exhaust.

As the piston moves up and down, a crank converts its movement to the rotary motion of the crankshaft, which powers the car's gears so the car wheels move. The intake of air and fuel and the removal of exhaust gases are controlled by **valves**, which are moved up and down by rotating cams.

UNDER PRESSURE

1 Pull the head of the pump out—this sucks air into the pump.

2 Cover the end where the air comes out with your hands.

Why does the air and fuel mixture heat up when the piston compresses it?

YOU WILL NEED:

✔ A bicycle tire pump
✔ Strong arms (or an adult helper)

3 Push the plunger in as hard as you can. If you need help, ask an adult.

4 Remove your hand from the air exit. Repeat steps 2 and 3 a few times.

5 Notice what happens to the air exit end of the pump.

HOW DOES IT WORK?

The heat you feel is the result of air molecules bashing into one another and bouncing off the walls of the pump. When you push the pump plunger, you're forcing all the molecules into a smaller **volume**, which makes them move faster. As a result, this area feels hotter.

warm

before

hot

after

IN FACT...

TYPES OF ENGINES

1) A diesel engine doesn't need a spark to ignite its diesel fuel. The heat caused by the piston compressing the fuel and air mixture is enough.
2) Internal combustion engines don't use all the potential energy in gas. No more than half of the energy is used to rotate the crankshaft. Half, or even three-quarters, of the energy is wasted as heat.
3) Hybrid cars combine an internal combustion engine with an electric **motor**. They save gas and reduce **pollution** from exhaust gases.

WHO WAS DIESEL?

Rudolf Diesel (1858–1913) was a German mechanical engineer who developed the diesel engine in the 1890s.

MOTORS ON THE MOVE

Automotive engineers work on the design and testing of cars, trucks, and motorcycles. They find ways to make them go fast, but still be safe. Let's check out a car's steering and gears. How do these parts keep the car on track?

→ what's the BIG idea?

HOW DOES A CAR DRIVE?

A car's steering column has **pivoted joints** that ensure that ups and downs on the road don't affect the steering. Most cars steer using a rack and pinion system where the axle meets the steering column.

Like bicycles, cars use gears to control the torque (turning force) that turns their wheels. In a car, this is called a transmission system.

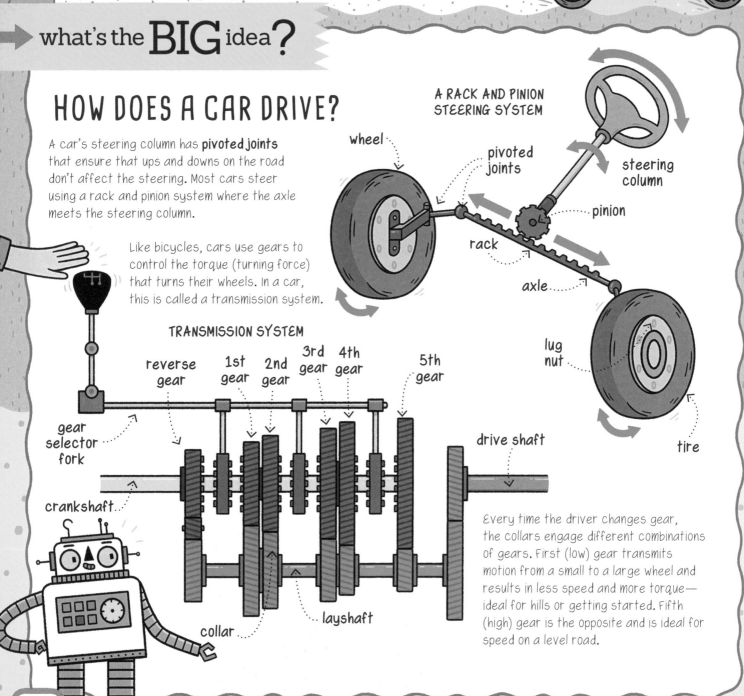

A RACK AND PINION STEERING SYSTEM

- wheel
- pivoted joints
- steering column
- pinion
- rack
- axle
- lug nut
- tire

TRANSMISSION SYSTEM

- reverse gear
- 1st gear
- 2nd gear
- 3rd gear
- 4th gear
- 5th gear
- drive shaft
- gear selector fork
- crankshaft
- collar
- layshaft

Every time the driver changes gear, the collars engage different combinations of gears. First (low) gear transmits motion from a small to a large wheel and results in less speed and more torque—ideal for hills or getting started. Fifth (high) gear is the opposite and is ideal for speed on a level road.

GEARING UP FOR SPEED

Now it's your turn to make a transmission system. All you'll need are a few simple materials and a little muscle power.

YOU WILL NEED:

- ✔ An adult helper
- ✔ A small cardboard box
- ✔ Two different-sized plastic bottle caps with ridged sides
- ✔ Scissors
- ✔ A metal skewer
- ✔ Two thin wooden dowels
- ✔ A ruler

1 Cut off the top and a side of the box.

2 Ask an adult to make a hole in each cap with the skewer. They must be in the middle.

hole

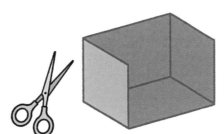

3 Make small holes in each side of the box. The holes should be exactly opposite each other. (You should check this with the ruler.)

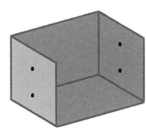

4 Push a dowel through one of the holes, then thread a cap onto the dowel. Push the dowel through the hole on the opposite side of the box.

dowel

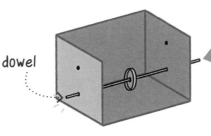

5 Repeat steps 3–4 with the other dowel and lid. The second dowel should be above the first dowel. The two caps must be able to turn against each other.

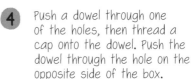

6 Rotate the lower dowel.

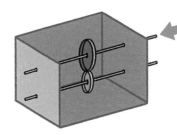

HOW DOES IT WORK?

The lower cap turns the upper cap like the gears in a transmission system. Now try gluing sandpaper around the gears. How does that affect the system? Does it create more friction? Try adding more gears of different sizes.

WHO WERE THE BENZES?

In 1885 Karl Benz (1844–1929) built the first practical car powered by the internal combustion engine. His wife Bertha Benz (1849–1944) was his organizer and funder. She even made the first long-distance car trip—without telling Karl!

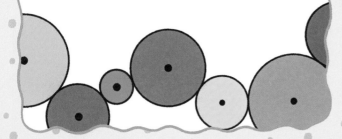

SHIP-SHAPED ENGINEERING

Ships and planes need engineers, too, so let's brave the waves with some ship designs. Have you ever wondered why ships are ship-shaped?

motor

stern

bow

TRY THIS AT HOME

WATCH THE WATER

Naval architectural engineers work on the design of marine vehicles and equipment. They need to consider how water flows across different shapes. This is called **hydrodynamics**. Let's investigate!

YOU WILL NEED:

✔ A large jug of water (you can add a few drops of food coloring so that the water shows up against the tray)

✔ A large, light-colored waterproof tray

✔ Modeling clay

✔ A ruler with metric and imperial measurements

✔ A sink or bathtub

① Make these three shapes (above) out of modeling clay. The sides should be about 1 cm high. Press them with the ruler until they are flat.

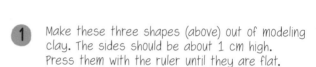

water

tray at angle

!

WARNING! VERY WET!

② Prop up the top of the tray at a slight angle, and carefully pour water down it so that the water flows around the shapes. Do this over a sink or in a bathtub.

HOW DOES IT WORK?

The water flows most easily around the boat shape and least easily around the square shape. As a ship moves forward, friction with the water creates a force called **drag** that slows it down. The **streamlined** ship shape reduces drag and allows the ship to go faster. Think about when these shapes may be used for different purposes in the ocean. Can you think of examples of when a square shape may be useful in water?

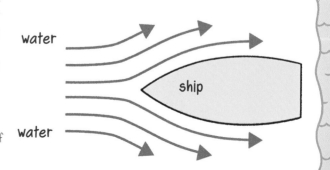

water

ship

water

42

STEERING CLEAR

Being streamlined and fast is fine—if you're sailing in a straight line. But what happens when you want to change course?

YOU WILL NEED:

✔ A piece of thick cardboard

✔ A ruler with metric and imperial measurements

✔ A pencil

✔ Scissors

✔ 4 in (10 cm) of thread

✔ Thick cardstock

✔ A toothpick

✔ Waterproof tape

✔ A bathtub

1 Draw and cut out a boat shape from the thick cardboard. Wrap tape around it to make it more watertight.

12 cm (4 1/2 in)

4.5 cm (1 3/4 in)

2 Tape the thread to the front of the boat.

thread

tape

3 Push the toothpick through the boat no more than 1/2 in (1 cm) from the center of its back edge.

1 1/2 in (4 cm) 1 1/2 in (4 cm)

1 1/2 in (4 cm)

fold

4 Draw and cut out this shape (right) from thick cardstock and fold it on the dotted line. This is your boat's **rudder** and **tiller**. Tape the two halves of the rudder together.

5 Wrap the tiller around the toothpick, and secure it with tape.

tiller

rudder

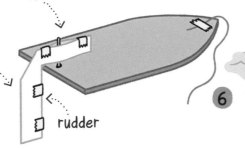

6 Fill the bathtub, and tow your boat in a straight line using the thread. Next, rotate the toothpick to turn the rudder to one side. Gently tow the boat again.

HOW DOES IT WORK?

As the tiller moves left, the rudder turns right and water pushes back against its right side. This forces the rudder and the rest of the boat around to the right. If you steer to the right, the boat moves to the left.

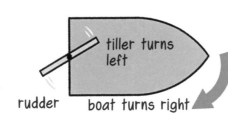

tiller turns left

rudder

boat turns right

SINKING OR HOVERING?

Not all boats float on water. Some hover over water or travel under it. How can that be? Let's try some experimental engineering.

TRY THIS AT HOME

MAKE A SINKING SUB

Submarines can dive down deep under the water. Here's an easy sinking submarine model you can test without getting your toes wet.

YOU WILL NEED:

- ✔ An adult helper
- ✔ A plastic bottle
- ✔ A bendy straw
- ✔ Water (or bathtub)
- ✔ Waterproof tape
- ✔ Heavy coins
- ✔ Modeling clay
- ✔ Plastic tubing
- ✔ A skewer

1 Ask an adult helper to make four holes in the side of the bottle with a skewer.

2 Tape a heavy coin to either end of the bottle, as shown.

3 Put the shortest part of the straw into the bottle opening. Seal it with modeling clay. Or you can ask an adult to make a hole in the bottle cap that is big enough for the straw to go through.

4 Attach some plastic tubing to the end of the straw if you want your submarine to go deeper.

5 Place your submarine in water. It will start to sink. Blow through the tube, and your submarine will start to rise again.

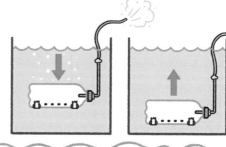

HOW DOES IT WORK?

The plastic bottle works in a similar way to a submarine. A submarine contains water tanks. When the tanks are full of water, the submarine is heavy and sinks to the seabed. When the tanks are emptied and filled with air, the submarine becomes lighter than the water around it and rises to the surface. The holes at the bottom of your submarine let water in, and it sinks. But when you blow air into it, it begins to rise.

HOVER AWAY

Why not whizz over the waves and dry land on a carpet of air? All you need is a hovercraft.

YOU WILL NEED:

- ✔ An adult helper
- ✔ An unwanted CD
- ✔ Wide packing tape
- ✔ A push pin
- ✔ Glue
- ✔ A plastic bottle with a sport cap
- ✔ Tape
- ✔ A balloon

WARNING! SHARP PIN

1 Stick packing tape over the hole in the CD.

packing tape

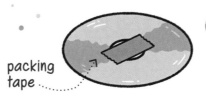

2 Ask an adult to prick six holes in the tape with the pin.

push pin

bottle cap

3 With adult help, glue the bottle top over the six small holes.

glue

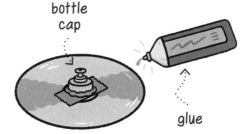

4 Inflate the balloon until it's saggy. Then blow it up again, and roll its neck over the bottle cap. You may need to secure the neck with tape.

5 Ensure the bottle cap valve is open, and place the CD on a smooth surface.

smooth surface

HOW DOES IT WORK?

Air from the balloon pushes through the small holes under the CD. It lifts the CD, reducing friction so that your model floats like a hovercraft. Try varying the size of the holes. Now try floating your hovercraft on a rougher surface. What happens?

HOW DOES A HOVERCRAFT WORK?

On a real hovercraft, the engine drives powerful lift fans that suck air under the bottom of the craft. The compressed air lifts the hovercraft and allows it to travel over land or water with little friction.

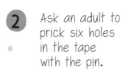
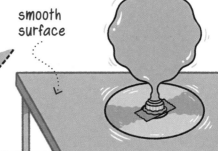

AWESOME AIRCRAFT

Wouldn't it be great to know how to build a plane and soar through the clouds! But first let's be an aeronautical (aircraft) engineer and figure out how planes fly.

what's the BIG idea?

HOW DO PLANES FLY?

Planes fly due to a combination of forces. In level flight at a constant speed, all four forces are perfectly balanced.

FORCES THAT AFFECT FLIGHT

The force of lift is the result of **air pressure.** The curved shape of a wing, known as airfoil, ensures that air passes more quickly over its upper surface than its lower surface. The air pressure under the wing is then higher than the air above the wing, resulting in the wing lifting the plane. The exact angles of the wings vary depending on the type of aircraft.

4. Lift, produced by the wings as they move through the air, pushes the the plane up.

4.

3.

Thrust, produced by the propellers, pushes the plane forward.

1.

Gravity pulls the plane down.

2.

Drag, or air resistance, pulls the plane backward.

airflow

Airfoil

ARE YOU A HIGH FLYER?

Here's a real challenge, engineers. Can you build a plane from one straw—and two pieces of paper? Yes, really!

YOU WILL NEED:

✔ Strong paper or thin cardstock

✔ A pencil

✔ Scissors

✔ A straight plastic straw

✔ Tape

✔ A ruler with metric and imperial measurements

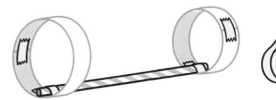

1 Draw two rectangles on the paper to the sizes shown, and cut them out.

1 in (2.5 cm)

6 ½ in (17 cm)

1 in (2.5 cm)

4 ½ in (11 cm)

2 Curl each piece into a loop with a 1 cm overlap. Try to make each loop as round as you can. Secure each loop with a 1 in (2.5 cm) length of tape.

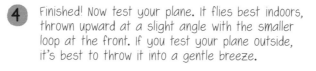

3 If necessary, cut the straw down to 8 in (20 cm), then stick it between the loops using 1 in (2 cm) pieces of tape on the inside of each loop.

4 Finished! Now test your plane. It flies best indoors, thrown upward at a slight angle with the smaller loop at the front. If you test your plane outside, it's best to throw it into a gentle breeze.

HOW DOES IT WORK?

It might not look like a plane, but it does fly like one! The loops act like wings providing lift and the streamlined shape reduces drag. And as a plane flies faster, it gets more lift. You could build a second plane and have a distance flying contest! Why not experiment by:

a) Adding more loops?
b) Using different materials?

Can you add a paper clip or two as cargo? Can you figure out where to attach the clips? Write down how far your plane goes each time and any other observations.

IN FACT...

Engineers are experimenting with unmanned planes called drones. These small planes can be radio-controlled or operate using their own onboard computer systems.

WHIRLING WINGS

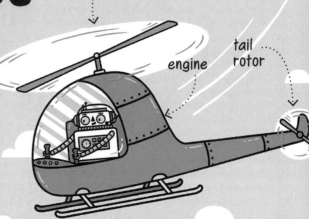

main rotor blades

engine

tail rotor

Helicopters are incredible machines, able to hover or turn in a moment. They have rotors (airfoil-shaped spinning blades) that produce lift and thrust. The pilot tilts the rotors to steer in any direction.

TRY THIS AT HOME

MAKE A PINWHEEL

In this experiment you can make some spinning rotors of your own.

YOU WILL NEED:

✔ An adult helper

✔ A 7 x 7-in (18 x 18-cm) square piece of paper (can be colored)

✔ A push pin

✔ Scissors

✔ Glue

✔ A pencil

✔ A dowel or straw

⚠️ WARNING! SHARP PIN!

1 Fold the paper corner to corner and then unfold it again.

2 Make a mark about $1/3$ down from the center on each of the folds.

3 Cut along the diagonal folded lines, but stop at the marks.

4 Bring all four points into the center and glue them together.

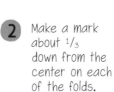

5 Push the map pin through all the layers at the centre holding the paper in place. Wiggle it a little to increase the size of the hole slightly. Ask an adult for help.

6 Stick the pin onto the top of a dowel.

HOW DOES IT WORK?

A helicopter's rotors turn to move air and create upward thrust, but your pinwheel is turned by moving air. It is also your breath, rather than an engine, that is powering it. How quickly do the blades spin? Try blowing from another angle. Where is it most effective? Try blowing with a hairdryer, and write down your results.

7 Turn the pinwheel. You can also try blowing it.

GIVE IT A WHIRL

Let's make a simple helicopter—it's not a full-size helicopter, but every engineering genius has to start somewhere!

YOU WILL NEED:

- ✔ An adult helper
- ✔ Thick paper
- ✔ Scissors
- ✔ A ruler
- ✔ A paper clip
- ✔ A pencil

WARNING! BEWARE HEIGHTS!

1 Cut the paper to 8 1/4 in (21 cm) long and 3 1/2 in (9 cm) wide.

3½ in (9 cm)

8¼ in (21 cm)

3½ in (9 cm)

3½ in (9 cm)

1¼ in (3 cm)

2 Draw this shape on the paper and cut it out.

1¼ in (3 cm)

3 Fold the shape along the dotted lines to make rotors.

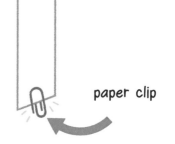

paper clip

4 Add the paper clip as shown.

5 Ask an adult for help, and try dropping your helicopter from up high!

HOW DOES IT WORK?

The wings on the "T" shape spin like helicopter rotors! Hopefully your helicopter made a safe landing. Why not draw a 12-in (30-cm) circle on a piece of paper and practice your landing skills?

WHO WAS DA VINCI?

Leonardo da Vinci (1452—1519) was an Italian inventor and artist who designed a "Helical Air Screw," which rotated, pushing on air to create flight —similar to today's helicopters. Da Vinci used the shape for other inventions and designs as well.

da Vinci's "Helical Air Screw"

JOIN THE GREEN TEAM

As a top agricultural engineer, you might find yourself designing equipment for farms. This could mean everything from constructing buildings for livestock to designing systems for watering crops.

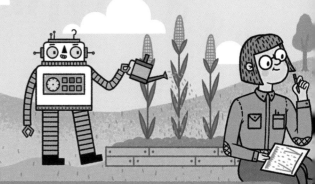

GROW WITH THE FLOW

Using channels for watering plants is known as irrigation. Irrigation systems have been used by humans for thousands of years. They are vital in areas that don't receive much rainfall. Here's a way you can design your own irrigation system.

YOU WILL NEED:

- ✔ An adult helper
- ✔ A large cardboard box
- ✔ Water
- ✔ Clean potting compost
- ✔ A trowel
- ✔ At least 6½ ft (2 m) of clear narrow plastic tubing
- ✔ Two large plastic liquid containers
- ✔ A ruler
- ✔ Waterproof tape
- ✔ A nail
- ✔ Scissors
- ✔ Plastic wrap
- ✔ A push pin
- ✔ Gardening gloves
- ✔ Cress seeds
- ✔ A garbage bag

1. First, draw a plan of your experiment. It's best to do this activity outside because it can get wet! Ideally, you should find an area for one of the containers that is raised.

2. Cut down the box sides to about 2 in (5 cm). You may want to line it with a garbage bag to contain moisture.

2 in (5 cm)

3. With your gloves on, fill your box with 1 in (2.5 cm) of compost.

compost

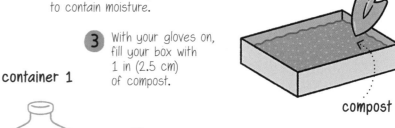

container 1

4. Ask an adult to make a small hole in container 1 with the nail. Enlarge the hole until it's big enough to hold the tube tightly. Insert the tubing and wrap waterproof tape around the outside of the container to help seal the tubing entry point.

5. Make a hole in one corner of the box about ¼ in (0.5 cm) above the compost and push the tubing through. Loop it back and forth over the compost to the far corner of the box. If the tubing doesn't stay on the soil, you can weigh it down with stones. Make a hole in the opposite side of the box and push the tubing through.

0.5 cm (¼ in) above compost

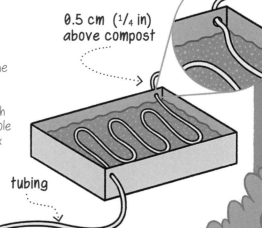

tubing

WARNING! SHARP PIN AND NAIL. BANDAGE ANY CUTS BEFORE WORKING WITH SOIL AND USE GLOVES

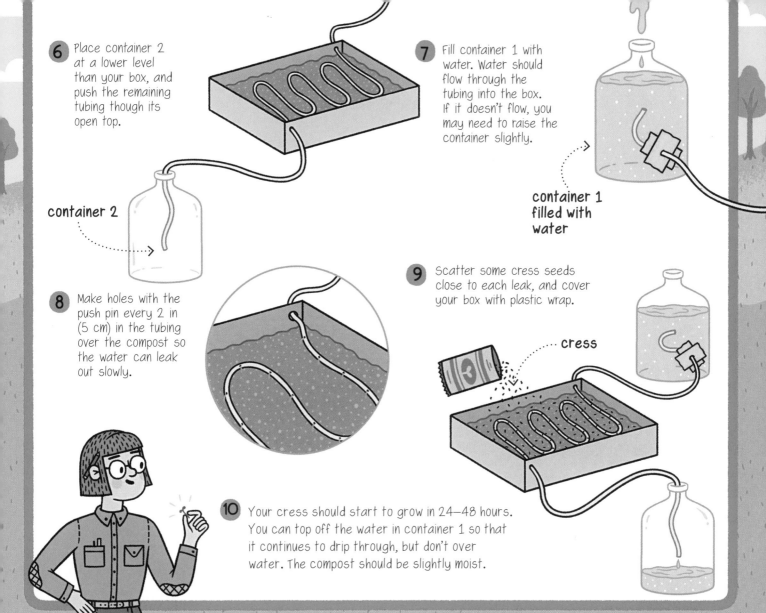

6 Place container 2 at a lower level than your box, and push the remaining tubing though its open top.

container 2

7 Fill container 1 with water. Water should flow through the tubing into the box. If it doesn't flow, you may need to raise the container slightly.

container 1 filled with water

8 Make holes with the push pin every 2 in (5 cm) in the tubing over the compost so the water can leak out slowly.

9 Scatter some cress seeds close to each leak, and cover your box with plastic wrap.

cress

10 Your cress should start to grow in 24–48 hours. You can top off the water in container 1 so that it continues to drip through, but don't over water. The compost should be slightly moist.

HOW DOES IT WORK?

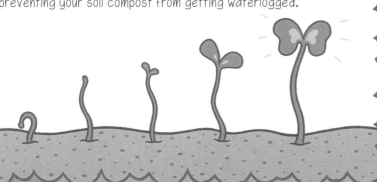

Your compost box is at a higher level than container 2, so gravity pulls the water downward through the tube. The pressure from the water traveling downward means the water continues to work its way through the tube to the opposite side of the box. The small holes in the tubing provide just enough water to keep the compost moist so your seeds can grow. Container 2 absorbs the excess water that runs straight through the tube, preventing your soil compost from getting waterlogged.

WHO WAS BOSE?

Jagadish Chandra Bose (1858–1937) was an Indian physicist and **biologist** who studied the **cells** of plants and argued that plants had the ability to feel pain and affection.

EXTREME CLEAN

The job of an environmental engineer is not just to clean up what has been polluted in our environment, but to help us reduce what we use and to dispose of it wisely. Let's check this out in more detail.

TRY THIS AT HOME

IT'S IN THE AIR

Nature needs our help to reduce pollution. Consider the air we breathe—is it really as clean as you think it is? Let's take a look!

YOU WILL NEED:

- ✔ An adult helper
- ✔ Two paper plates
- ✔ A hole puncher
- ✔ String
- ✔ A ruler
- ✔ Scissors
- ✔ Petroleum jelly

WARNING! BEWARE HEIGHTS!

1 Make two holes in each plate with a hole puncher.

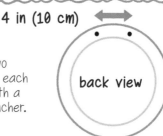

4 in (10 cm)

back view

knot

front view

2 Cut two 12-in (30-cm) lengths of string, and thread one string through the holes on the back of one plate, and tie the ends together. Repeat with the other string and plate. Cover the front of each plate with petroleum jelly.

3 Ask an adult to help you hang your pollution catchers from trees or other objects out of reach of pets. Hang one pollution catcher next to a busy road and one in a yard away from traffic. Leave them for 2–4 weeks.

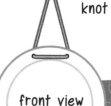

HOW DOES IT WORK?

Both plates will look dirty, but the plate closest to the road is likely to be the dirtiest. It will have been exposed to more pollution, such as tiny unburnt fuel particles from car exhaust.

CLEARLY BETTER

The germs in polluted water can make people ill. We need environmental engineers to clean things up. Let's make a start.

YOU WILL NEED:

- ✔ An adult helper
- ✔ A 2-liter plastic bottle
- ✔ A ruler
- ✔ Cotton balls
- ✔ Fine sand
- ✔ Coarse sand
- ✔ Gravel
- ✔ Water
- ✔ Tape

WARNING! DON'T DRINK! SHARP EDGE OF BOTTLE!

1 With help from an adult, cut the bottle in half (the top half should be at least 6 in (15 cm), not counting the neck. Add some tape along the bottom edges of each bottle half to reduce sharpness.

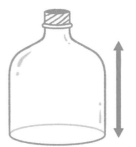

6 in (15 cm)

2 Layer the materials in the top half of the bottle as shown. Each layer should be about 1 in (2.5 cm) thick. Place the upturned half into the bottom half of the bottle.

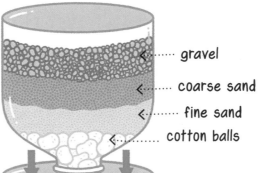

gravel
coarse sand
fine sand
cotton balls

bottom of bottle

dirty water

3 Mix some dirt with water and slowly pour it into the top of your newly made filter.

HOW DOES IT WORK?

The water in the container at the bottom should look fairly clean, BUT DON'T DRINK THE WATER—it may contain germs! The layers of materials act as a filter, letting water through but blocking some of the bigger pollutants. Wash out the base and test out other "pollutants" to filter out of water, such as coffee granules, flour, or cooking oil mixed in water. (You may find that traces of the last pollutants come through, too.) What types of things would not be removed with a filter as simple as this one?

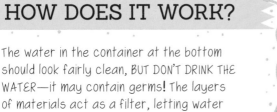

WHO WAS HIPPOCRATES?

Hippocrates (c. 460 B.C.E.– c. 370 B.C.E.) was an ancient Greek doctor who is sometimes called the "Father of Medicine." He designed a simple water filter out of a cloth bag to purify water for use on his patients.

SUPER SUBSTANCES

The clothes we wear, the food we consume, and the energy we use all depend on chemical engineering. The materials that these products are made of are developed often by chemical engineers in chemical plants.

what's the BIG idea?

HOW DOES A CHEMICAL PLANT WORK?

Chemical plants are factories where raw chemicals are transformed into useful substances. Chemical plants can specialize in different products, such as oil, plastic, and food. But they all depend on chemical engineers to design them and keep them running.

1. Vessel to store chemicals at high or low pressures and temperatures.

2. Chemicals are mixed and heated in chemical **reactors** to trigger **chemical reactions** that make a new substance. Some substances might be dissolved or separated into more basic molecules.

3. The chemical reactors and vessels are connected by pipes.

5. **Pumps** (see p. 58) keep liquids moving.

4. Valves (see p. 58) ensure that liquids can only move one way.

6. Machines called compressors keep chemicals under pressure.

GREEN EGG TIME

To get a sense of what goes on in a chemical plant, let's cook up something weird. Cooking can be **chemistry**, too. You can eat the result —but only if you're brave enough!

YOU WILL NEED:

- ✔ An adult helper
- ✔ An egg
- ✔ A head of red cabbage
- ✔ A pot
- ✔ A frying pan
- ✔ A wooden spoon
- ✔ Vegetable oil
- ✔ Two measuring cups or containers
- ✔ Water
- ✔ A stove or hot plate

egg white

yolk

WARNING! BEWARE HEAT!

red cabbage

1 Peel off about a quarter of the leaves from the red cabbage, and place them in the pot.

2 Cover the cabbage with a very little bit of water. Get an adult to boil the cabbage for 5–10 minutes or until the water is deep purple.

3 Gently break the egg into the jug. Don't break the yolk. Scoop the yolk out with the spoon, and put it in the egg shell.

4 Mix the remaining egg white with a little cabbage water.

5 Add a little oil to the frying pan. With adult help, heat the oil and add the egg white. Gently place the egg yolk on top of the white and fry the egg.

HOW DOES IT WORK?

Your fried egg white isn't white and it isn't red—it's GREEN! Red cabbage contains a substance called **anthocyanin** that changes color when it mixes with substances that are acids or **bases**. Egg white is a very weak base. Now imagine a chemical plant making green eggs on an industrial scale!

IN FACT...

DID YOU KNOW?

Most known substances have been carefully tested, but we are constantly finding new and interesting things about them, and sometimes unexpected results! Chemical engineers figure out ways to make all these products, while helping to manage the world's **resources**, protecting the **environment**, and ensuring health and safety standards are met.

MEDICAL MECHANICS

Engineers don't just fix machines, they also help to fix us! They design and work with machines that help to heal and study the human body.

what's the BIG idea?

BIOMEDICAL ENGINEERING

Biomedical engineers develop machines, medicines, and equipment to identify and treat disease and to keep us healthy. This can be anything from glasses to sports equipment. They also design new artificial body parts, called prosthetics, to take the place of damaged or diseased body parts.

WHAT'S GOING ON?

HOW DOES A MEDICAL VENTILATOR WORK?

A medical ventilator is a machine that helps a patient breathe when they're having problems breathing on their own.

2. The air travels through a tube to the lungs.

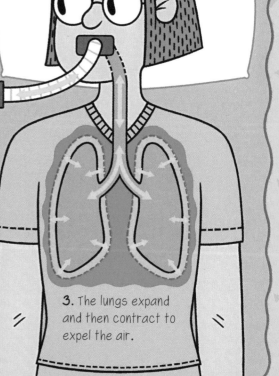

1. An electric pump forces air and **oxygen** into the patient's lungs. The air is warmed and a computer controls the pump.

4. The air travels back to the machine.

3. The lungs expand and then contract to expel the air.

MAKE A MODEL VENTILATOR

Here's how to make a simple machine that works a bit like a ventilator!

YOU WILL NEED:

- ✔ A 2-liter plastic bottle
- ✔ Two balloons
- ✔ Two bendy straws
- ✔ Duct tape
- ✔ Modeling clay

1 Partially blow up and release the balloons to make them looser.

2 Bend the straws, attach a balloon to each one, and secure them with duct tape.

3 Tape the straws together to form a "Y" shape.

4 Place the straws in the bottle, and secure them with modeling clay around the opening of the bottle.

5 Now try blowing into the straws, and watch what happens.

HOW DOES IT WORK?

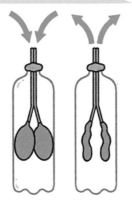

Your balloons and bottle act a bit like a ventilator. The balloons are like your lungs —they inflate when you blow air into them and deflate when you stop blowing.

WHO WAS DRINKER?

Philip Drinker (1894–1972) was a chemical and medical engineer who invented one of the first widely used mechanical breathing machines, known as the iron lung.

IN FACT...

ARTIFICIAL HEART

Biomedical engineers design artificial hearts that can take over for a patient's real heart for a few months. In 1949, surgeons in the United States built an artificial heart from parts of kids' toys!

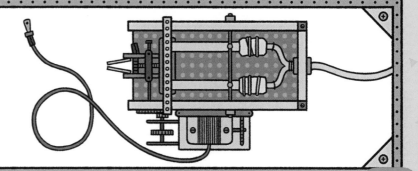

WONDERFUL WATERWORKS

Fluid engineering is all about working with liquids. Moving liquids have a lot of energy. Let's look at how engineers harness the power of liquids.

 **what's the BIG idea?**

LIQUIDS

The molecules in a liquid are more densely packed than they are in a gas. This is why a container of water weighs more than a container of air. Engineers investigate what happens when a liquid is heated or compressed (squashed into a small area).

Liquids can be controlled using...
* pipes
* pumps (devices that raise, compress, or transport liquids)
* valves (parts that open, shut, or partly close to control the flow of water, for instance in pipes)
* dams (barriers built in rivers or streams to hold water)

These make liquids flow smoothly—for instance, to irrigate crops, fill canals, and heat homes through radiators.

TRY THIS AT HOME

TELL THE TIME WITH WATER!

Here's an old device that dates back to at least 1500 B.C.E. Yes, engineers, you really can use water to tell the time!

YOU WILL NEED:

- ✓ An adult helper
- ✓ A marker
- ✓ A 2-liter plastic bottle
- ✓ Scissors
- ✓ Tape
- ✓ A nail
- ✓ A watch with a second hand
- ✓ Water
- ✓ A ruler

WARNING! SHARP NAIL!

dotted line ....   cut

2 Ask an adult to help you make a small hole in the bottle cap with the nail. Replace the cap and position the top half of the bottle upside down into the lower half. Make sure the hole in the cap is small or you may find the water flows out too quickly.

1 Mark a dotted line on the bottle a little over half way up. Ask an adult to cut around this line, and add some tape to smooth off the edges.

hole ....

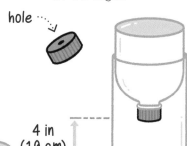

4 in (10 cm)

3 Fill the top half of the bottle with water, and mark the water level in the bottom half every minute until the top half is empty. Use the ruler to measure how much water leaks each minute.

HOW DOES IT WORK?

Your water clock works because the water leaks through the hole at a predictable rate. Once you know what this rate is, you can figure out the time from it. The leak is faster at first because when the top half of the bottle is full, the water pressure is greater. This is one of the basic ideas of water engineering.

Water clocks are some of the oldest ways to measure time. Over two thousand years ago, the ancient Greeks called water clocks clepsydras. They developed water clocks that had stoppers so they could control the rate of the water passing through and make timekeeping more accurate.

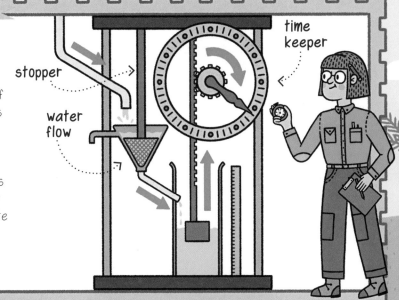

stopper

water flow

time keeper

WHAT'S GOING ON?

HOW DOES HYDROELECTRIC POWER WORK?

Hydroelectric power is electricity produced by the energy of moving water. About 16 percent of the world's electricity is produced by hydroelectric power.

1. Water falls from a higher **reservoir** to a lower reservoir by the force of gravity.
2. The force of falling water spins blades on a machine called a **turbine.**
3. The energy produced by the turbine is turned into electricity by a **generator.**

Higher reservoir

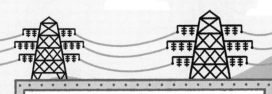

Lower reservoir

IN FACT

WATER MILLS

A water wheel is an ancient mechanism for harnessing the power of water. It's been used to pump water, grind grain, and crush rock for metal mining.

rotating cams lift and drop stampers

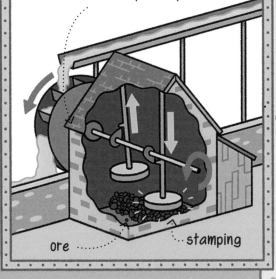

ore

stamping

BIOENGINEERING

Bioengineering develops inventions related to livings things. We have seen that engineering methods can be used in medicine, but they can also be used to make new things from animals and plant parts.

what's the BIG idea?

USING MICROBES

One type of bioengineering uses living microbes (tiny microscopic creatures, such as **bacteria**) to create useful products, such as fuel and food. The fuel ethanol can be made from altering the cells (building blocks) of bacteria and mixing them with plant waste.

IN FACT...

GENES AND GENETIC ENGINEERING

All living things are made of tiny building blocks called cells. Genes are found inside cells. They act as instructions for how a cell should behave. Genes are made of a substance called **deoxyribonucleic acid (DNA)**, which is shaped like a twisted ladder—scientists call this shape a double helix. Each strand of the ladder is made up of pairs of chemicals called bases.

A gene is a shorter length of DNA that tells a cell how to develop and what it should do. Genetic engineering (or GM) involves altering the code in a gene so that the cell does something else—like making a useful substance.

DNA

pairs of base chemicals

WHO WAS WEIZMANN?

Chaim Ariel Weizmann (1874–1952) was the first president of Israel and also a biochemist. He developed the process of making ethanol from bacteria.

MAKING MICROBE GAS

Welcome to the biotech business, engineers! We're about to use microbes to make some gas.

YOU WILL NEED:

- ✔ A 500 ml plastic bottle
- ✔ A measuring cup
- ✔ A balloon
- ✔ A teaspoon
- ✔ A wooden spoon
- ✔ Sugar
- ✔ A packet of dried yeast
- ✔ Water

1 Add ¾ cup of warm tap water to the measuring cup. It shouldn't be too hot or it will kill the yeast.

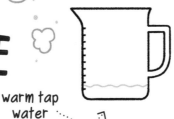

warm tap water

sugar

2 Add one teaspoon of sugar. Keep stirring until the sugar dissolves.

yeast

3 Stir yeast into the cup until it is well mixed. Carefully pour the mixture from the cup into the bottle.

bottle

balloon

measuring cup

4 Blow up and release the balloon to loosen it. Stretch the balloon neck over the bottle neck, and leave your experiment in a warm place for 20 minutes.

HOW DOES IT WORK?

The balloon is slightly inflated with **carbon dioxide** gas. Yeasts are tiny living things related to fungi. They consist of cells that feed on sugar and produce carbon dioxide. (Human cells do the same thing, which is why we breathe out more carbon dioxide than we breathe in from the air.)

Try the same experiment using hotter and colder water. Use a thermometer to measure the temperature of the water. At what temperature is the yeast most active? At what temperatures is it unable to blow up the balloon? What do you think this tells you?

yeast granules

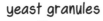

IN FACT...
DID YOU KNOW?

1. Genetically engineered bacteria are used to make vital drugs, such as insulin, for people with diabetes. People with diabetes have levels of sugar in their blood that are too high.

2. Genetic engineering has produced plants that glow in the dark. Scientists have even created glow-in-the-dark animals!

3. Yeast has been used in breadmaking for thousands of years. When the yeast produces carbon dioxide as the bread is baked, the bread begins to rise. It's one of the oldest forms of biotechnology!

BRIGHT SPARK ENGINEERS

Picture this: Your home has lost power—it's dark, cold, and there are no gadgets to have fun with. Nightmare, huh? Let's give three cheers to the electrical engineers who keep the current flowing!

→ what's the **BIG** idea?

WHAT IS ELECTRICAL ENGINEERING?

Electrical engineers use electricity and the science of electromagnetism (see p. 12) to generate electricity and design electric machines. This includes the field of electronics, which means controlling the flow of electrons (see p. 12) in an electric circuit. It also branches into electrical devices, including computers.

TRY THIS AT HOME

BUILD A CIRCUIT

Electricity can flow in a wire if it has somewhere to go. This is the purpose of an electrical circuit—as you're about to find out.

YOU WILL NEED:

- ✔ An adult helper
- ✔ A small 2-volt flashlight bulb
- ✔ Two AA 1.5-volt batteries
- ✔ Tape
- ✔ Wire strippers
- ✔ Electrical wire (about 12 in/30 cm)

⚠ **WARNING! BATTERIES MAY GET HOT!**

1 Ask an adult to strip ¼ in (0.5 cm) of plastic covering off each end of the wire.

2 Tape one end of the wire to the base (negative end) of a battery.

negative end

positive end

3 Hold the base of the bulb on the positive end of the battery, and touch the other end of the wire to its metal side. The lightbulb should light.

4 Now tape the positive ends of the two batteries together. Hold the bulb on the negative end of the second battery, and again, touch the end of the wire to its metal side.

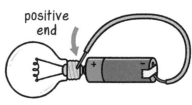

5 The lightbulb doesn't light! Now for your challenge! Because the bulb lit up at step 3, you know that your equipment is working. How will you change things to make the bulb light?

HOW DOES IT WORK?

The battery, wire, and bulb form a circuit for an electrical current to flow through. But the electrons in a circuit will only move from negative areas to positive areas. This means that the electrons are moving from areas where there are lots of them to areas where there aren't. To make the circuit work so the lightbulb lights, you have to connect the negative end of the second battery to the positive end of the first battery.

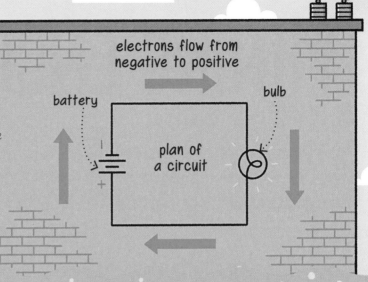

electrons flow from negative to positive

battery

bulb

plan of a circuit

WHAT'S GOING ON?

ELECTRIC MOTOR

Electric motors convert electrical energy into kinetic energy to make things move. You'll find them in everything from toys to real trains. An electric current is always surrounded by a **magnetic field** created by an electromagnetic force (p. 13). Inside an electric motor, a device called a commutator makes the current constantly change direction in a wire loop. The magnetic field around the loop changes direction too—pulling and pushing on the magnetic fields of the magnets on either side. This spins the loop around, generating power.

SPIN

wire loop

magnet   N   S   magnet

magnetic field

commutator

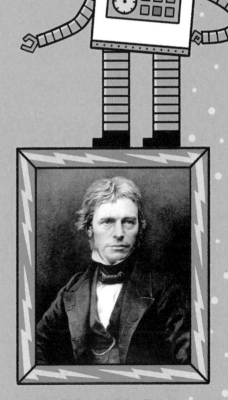

WHO WAS FARADAY?

Michael Faraday (1791–1867) was an English scientist who discovered how to produce an electric current from a magnetic field.

MINING ENGINEERING

Mining engineers are involved in finding new ways to extract valuable minerals from the earth. Grab your hard hats and let's go see what they're up to!

→ what's the BIG idea?

MINERALS

Minerals are natural occurring chemical **compounds**—they are made up of molecules that contain more than one type of atom. They're often found below ground. Useful minerals include coal and oil for energy, metals (such as iron), stone, salt and minerals used in medicines.

Quartz is a mineral made of silicon and oxygen in crystal form. It's used in the making of sand and glass.

TRY THIS AT HOME

DENSITY DATA

Sometimes minerals are difficult to tell apart. Engineers can differentiate between them by finding a mineral's **density** (or mass per unit volume).

YOU WILL NEED:

- ☑ A weighing scale
- ☑ A selection of large stones
- ☑ A bowl a little larger than the largest stone
- ☑ A measuring cup
- ☑ Water
- ☑ Paper
- ☑ A pencil
- ☑ A calculator
- ☑ A shallow container for the bowl to sit in

1 Weigh a stone, and write down its weight.

2 Fill the bowl to the brim with water, and place the stone in the water.

overflow container

3 Pour the water that overflows into the measuring cup. Write down the quantity of water.

4 To find the density of the stone, divide its weight by the quantity of water it pushes aside. For example:

A **100 g** stone pushing aside **20 ml** of water =
100 g divided by **20 ml** = 5 g

The density of your stone = 5 g / ml

5 Compare the density of the stones in your collection.

Weight is a measure of mass (except in space where there's little gravity!), and volume is equal to the amount of water an object pushes aside. Because each mineral has a different density, this test helps to tell them apart. Metallic minerals, such as gold, are denser than ordinary stones. This test can even show if a shiny yellow mineral is iron pyrite or genuine gold!

WHAT'S GOING ON?

HOW DOES A MINE WORK?

Mining engineers design and look after mines and their machinery. There are two main types of mining—surface and underground.

Both methods use machinery such as heavy drills to break open rock so that **ore** (rock-containing minerals) can be removed. Sometimes explosives are used instead. Elevators transport miners to the working areas. Conveyer belts, trucks, cranes, and mechanical shovels are needed to move the broken rock to the areas where the minerals are removed by crushing and grinding.

Let's take a look at a surface mine:

IN FACT...

FRACKING

Fracking is a way of extracting oil or gas from areas underground that are difficult to reach. Water, sand, and chemicals are injected into the rock at high pressure, allowing the gas to flow out to the surface. There is controversy surrounding this method because the chemicals can can create pollution and the process can cause small Earth tremors.

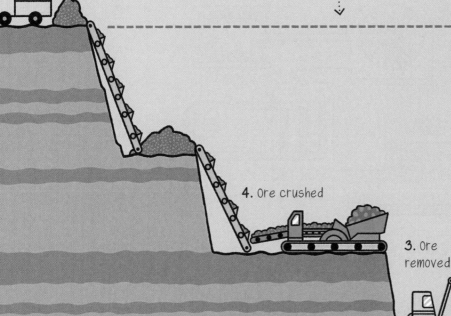

Surface level

5. Crushed ore taken for processing.

4. Ore crushed

1. Rock removed

2. Waste rock dumped

3. Ore removed

NUCLEAR POWER

Hidden away in the heart of an atom is the most awesome power in the known universe. But what is it? It has to do with splitting atoms into smaller parts. Let's investigate!

nucleus

radiation

what's the BIG idea?

POWER FROM ATOMS

Inside every atom is a nucleus consisting of particles called protons, neutrons, and electrons (see p. 12). In some atoms, the nucleus is unstable and loses energy in the form of radiation—high-energy electromagnetic waves and particles.

A nuclear power station has a reactor where these atoms are split in a controlled way. This reaction produces heat, which flows through water or gas. The hot water spins a spinining mechanism called a turbine, which then spins a generator to make electricity.

Nuclear engineers work on nuclear power projects, either building power stations or ensuring that the stations run safely. Safety is a big concern because although accidents are extremely rare, if radiation escapes, it can cause damage to the cells of living things.

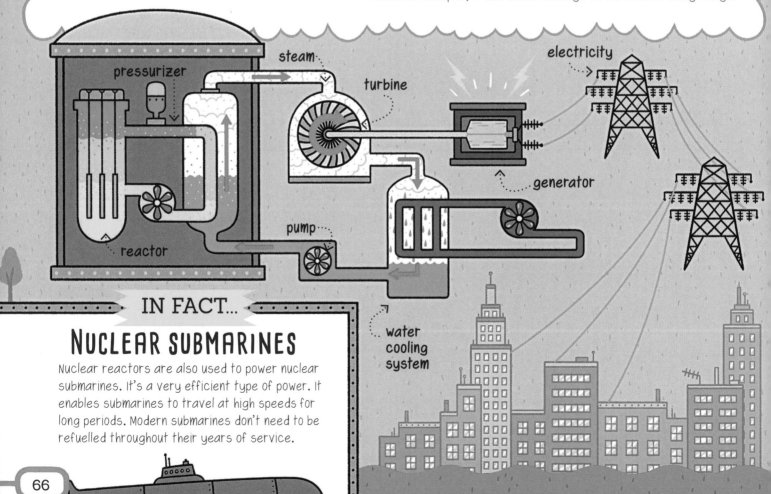

pressurizer

steam

turbine

electricity

generator

pump

reactor

water cooling system

IN FACT...

NUCLEAR SUBMARINES

Nuclear reactors are also used to power nuclear submarines. It's a very efficient type of power. It enables submarines to travel at high speeds for long periods. Modern submarines don't need to be refuelled throughout their years of service.

NUCLEAR POWER AND RADIATION

* The first submarine to sail under the North Pole was USS Nautilus in 1958. The super powerful submarine was powered by an on-board nuclear reactor.

* Uranium is a radioactive material that is found in the earth and used in nuclear power stations. Something that is radioactive has atoms that are unstable and give out radiation.

uranium ore

TRY THIS AT HOME

SHINING SCIENCE

Many nuclear engineers look for ways to protect people from radiation—and you can, too. Here's an experiment that's safe even if you are working with a giant nuclear reactor! We're talking about the sun!

YOU WILL NEED:

✔ Black cardstock or construction paper
✔ A colored pencil
✔ Sunscreen
✔ A sunny day

1 Draw a shape on the construction paper.

smear sunscreen

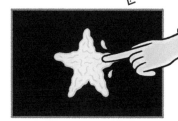

2 Collect a pea-sized ball of sunscreen on your fingertip, and smear it all over every part of your shape. Don't smear sunscreen outside your lines.

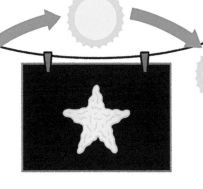

3 Leave the paper in the sun all day. You might need to move it around to ensure that it stays in the sunlight.

HOW DOES IT WORK?

The paper fades—except for the sunscreen covered shape. Unlike in a nuclear power station, atomic nuclei in the sun are fused (joined) rather than split. But like a nuclear power station, this releases heat and radiation.

Most of the sun's harmful radiation doesn't reach us, but waves of light called **ultraviolet light** do. This radiation causes sunburn and fades the paper. Depending on what kind of sunscreen it is, the sunscreen protects the paper by reflecting, blocking, or soaking up ultraviolet radiation.

ultraviolet light

CLUED-UP COMPUTING

OK, so you can switch on your favorite device
and open your favorite apps—but what's inside?
Here's your chance to get clued-up on computers!

what's the **BIG** idea?

HOW DOES A COMPUTER WORK?

A computer is a machine that performs certain tasks using numbers and words, and it stores information following a set of instructions called a program. Computer engineers design computers and write programs.

LEARN COMPUTER-SPEAK

Hardware = the actual machine and the machines you connect to it.

Software = programs stored in in the computer's memory.

CPU = Central Processing Unit (where information is organized)

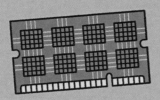

RAM = Random Access Memory (where information is stored temporarily)

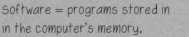

Input = hardware you use to put information into your computer, such as a keyboard and mouse.

Output = hardware to get information out of your computer, such as a printer.

This is what the main computer components are:

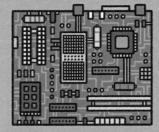

Motherboard—this is the board on which most of the other inside parts are set.

Power supply—computers need a power cord or a battery to operate.

CPU—or microprocessor. Processes (organizes and alters) information you put in according to the instructions in a computer program.

Hard drive—the computer's memory where programs and information are stored permanently.

DIGITAL MACHINES

Computers are digital machines. This means that information is stored and instructions given in a number system known as binary code made up of 1s or 0s. A 1 is a set **voltage** of electricity and 0 is nothing. One vital job computer software does is to translate between our words and binary code.

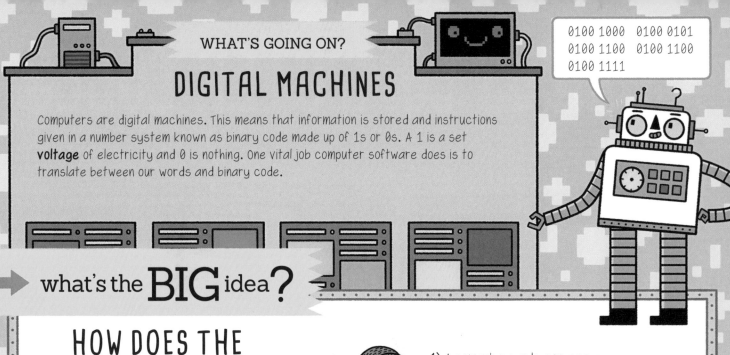

0100 1000   0100 0101
0100 1100   0100 1100
0100 1111

what's the BIG idea?

HOW DOES THE INTERNET WORK?

The Internet is a worldwide network linking electronic devices, such as computers and smartphones. Every device has an address called an IP (Internet Protocol) address. It allows one device to communicate with another over the Internet according to set rules. ....

1) A computer sends a message asking for a web page. The message is called a packet.

2) The packet is processed by routers and servers (large computers that sort out requests and deliveries of data) and guided across the world by **fiber optic cable** or **satellite**.

Every message on the Internet carries the sender's IP address, the IP address it is sent to, and instructions for assembling the packets. So even if a device is shared by people with different names and e-mail addresses, the information can get to the right place.

5) A computer assembles packets and shows a web page on screen.

3) An Internet server computer receives the message.

4) A web page is broken down into many packets and sent back in the same way.

CURIOUS COMPUTER CODES

We've seen that data in a computer is represented by a number system known as binary code. Computer engineers create these codes as part of computer programs. Computer programs are contained in a computer's software.

what's the BIG idea?

COMPUTER PROGRAMS

A computer program is a set of instructions written in a programming language. A computer's processor can't actually understand this, so other programs need to turn the instructions into on-off digital binary code. In a computer it's known as machine code.

TRY THIS AT HOME

WRITE YOUR NAME IN COMPUTER LANGUAGE

ASCII is a basic computer code. Its name stands for American Standard Code for Information Interchange. In ASCII, each letter and number becomes a binary code with 8 digits. Can you write your name in ASCII?

YOU WILL NEED:

- ✔ Graph paper
- ✔ A colored pencil
- ✔ A pencil

① Draw a box with eight squares across. The number of squares down depends on the number of letters in your name.

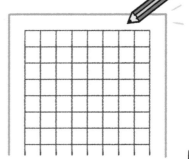

② Look up each letter in your name in the ASCII code table (right). Start your name on the first line of eight squares. Color in a square for each 1, but leave 0 squares blank.

ASCII CODE	
A	0100 0001
B	0100 0010
C	0100 0011
D	0100 0100
E	0100 0101
F	0100 0110
G	0100 0111
H	0100 1000
I	0100 1001
J	0100 1010
K	0100 1011
L	0100 1100
M	0100 1101
N	0100 1110
O	0100 1111
P	0101 0000
Q	0101 0001
R	0101 0010
S	0101 0011
T	0101 0100
U	0101 0101
V	0101 0110
W	0101 0111
X	0101 1000
Y	0101 1001
Z	0101 1010

CONGRATULATIONS! You've written your name in computer language! Why not design a banner using string and colored paper with your name in ASCII code?

0100 0011 0100 1111 0100 1110 0100 0111 0101 0010
0100 0001 0101 0100 0101 0101 0100 1100 0100 0001
0101 0100 0100 1001 0100 1111 0100 1110 0101 0011

TRY THIS AT HOME

MAKE A SECRET CODE SIGNALLER

Now that you've figured out ASCII, why not send secret messages to your engineer friends during a sleepover after lights out?

YOU WILL NEED:

- ✓ Cellophane (could be from a plastic folder)
- ✓ A black marker (to write on cellophane)
- ✓ A small bright flashlight

1 Draw an eight-square-wide grid on the cellophane. It needs as many boxes down as the letters in your code word. This box can be quite small—it's meant to be secret!

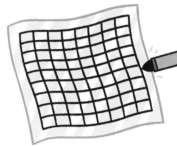

2 Using the ASCII code table, draw a black circle where there's a "0" in a box. Leave the "1" boxes empty.

3 Wait until dark. Make sure your friend has the code table. Hold the cellophane up and shine the flashlight on the front of it.

HOW DOES IT WORK?

Your message will project on the wall. Can your friend read it? How about you— can you read this message?

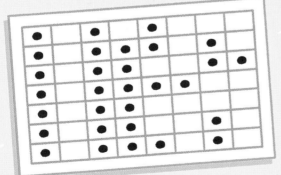

WHO WAS HOPPER?

Grace Hopper (1906–1992) was an American mathematician and rear admiral in the U.S. navy who was once a pioneer of computer programming and helped develop UNIVAC I, the first commercial computer.

THE ANSWERS ARE AT THE BACK OF THE BOOK

WATERY WILDERNESS

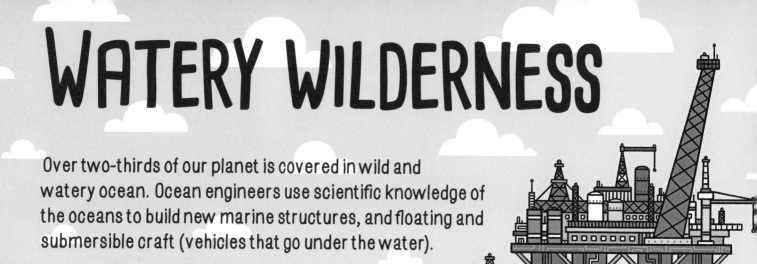

Over two-thirds of our planet is covered in wild and watery ocean. Ocean engineers use scientific knowledge of the oceans to build new marine structures, and floating and submersible craft (vehicles that go under the water).

what's the BIG idea?

COMBATING POLLUTION

One of the roles of an ocean engineer is to combat pollution of the oceans. A large amount of waste, from oil to garbage and chemicals to sewage, is dumped in the world's oceans every day. Pollution is harming the marine wildlife.

WHAT'S GOING ON?

ARTIFICIAL REEFS

Artificial (human-made) reefs are being built to encourage sea life. Coral reefs form in warm, coastal waters. They are formed from the mineral skeletons of living things called corals. Coral reefs are home to many types of wildlife, including fish, sponges, mussels, jellyfish, crabs, and sea urchins. Artificial reefs can be formed from solid structures, such as shipwrecks, onto which corals and other sea life attach.

UNDERWATER DISCOVERY

Ocean engineering has led to the development of equipment, such as submersibles, that take us deep into the ocean. We now know that the deep oceans have mountains, deep valleys, and vast plains. In 1977, the first hydrothermal vents were discovered. These vents gush out super hot, mineral-rich water. Water enters cracks in the earth's crust, is heated by hot, molten rock deep underground, and then spewed out into the ocean.

TRY THIS AT HOME

SINK OR SWIM?

Here's a simple experiment to discover how the salinity (saltiness) of water affects how things float.

YOU WILL NEED:

✔ Two clear bowls (or you can use drinking glasses)
✔ Warm water
✔ Salt
✔ Two eggs
✔ Food coloring
✔ A tablespoon

1 Pour some warm water into each bowl.

2 Add enough salt to one of the bowls to make the water murky white, and stir well until it all dissolves.

3 Place an egg in each bowl. What happens?

4 Take the eggs out of the bowls, and add a dash of food coloring to each bowl. What do you notice?

WHAT'S GOING ON?

SALTY OCEANS

What makes objects float in water? If an object is less dense than the water around it, it will float. This is called buoyancy. The world's oceans are full of salt water, which is denser than freshwater, so objects float more easily in seawater than in water elsewhere. The amount of salt in the oceans varies. In places where there is little rain (which provides freshwater) there tends to be more salt in the ocean.

HOW DOES IT WORK?

The egg in the water without salt sinks to the bottom of the bowl. That's because the density of the egg is greater than the density of the water. If you add salt to the water, it becomes more dense and the egg starts to float. The greater the amount of salt in the water, the better the egg will float. You can also try this experiment with pieces of potato instead of an egg. Do you notice a difference in the results?

ROCKET POWER

3... 2... 1... LIFT OFF!
What makes a rocket launch? What thrusts it into space? Hold onto your helmets, engineers—we're going to make a rocket and find out!

WHAT'S GOING ON?

HOW DO SPACE ROCKETS WORK?

On the launch pad, the rocket burns fuel, which turns into hot gas. The gas is forced DOWNWARD out of the rocket. According to Newton's Third Law of Motion, this downward force must produce an opposite force—so the rocket is pushed UPWARD.

burning fuel

rocket is forced upward

hot gas is blasted downward

EVERY ACTION HAS AN EQUAL AND OPPOSITE REACTION.

→ what's the BIG idea?

NEWTON'S THIRD LAW OF MOTION

Newton's Third Law of Motion explains that forces always occur in pairs, and every action has an equal and opposite reaction. For instance, a book lying on a table exerts a downward force on the table. Meanwhile, the table is exerting an equal upward force on the book—so the book stays still.

MAKE A JET PROPULSION ROCKET!

Do you want to make a rocket without an enormous explosion? You're in luck. We can force gas out of a rocket without burning fuel. We do need two of the same ingredients, though: gas and pressure (the pushing force that expels the gas). Our gas will be air, and we will use a balloon to create the pressure.

YOU WILL NEED:

- ✔ An adult helper
- ✔ A long party balloon
- ✔ Tape
- ✔ A straw
- ✔ Two chairs
- ✔ About 10 ft (3 m) of copper wire

1 Thread the wire through the straw and stretch it tight across a room. Tie it to two objects, for instance, between two chairs. The straw should be positioned at one end of the wire.

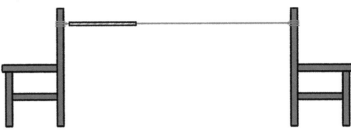

2 Blow into the balloon and release it to make it saggy. Blow it up fully and ask an adult to hold the neck in place.

3 Take the balloon to the wire, and while your helper is still holding the neck, tape the balloon to the straw. Make sure the neck is facing the nearest end of the wire.

4 Count "3,2,1," then tell your adult helper to let go of the balloon. watch what happens!

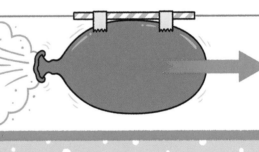

IN FACT

HOW DOES IT WORK?

When your rocket is released, air rushes out of the balloon in a powerful forward motion called thrust. The thrust comes from the energy of the balloon forcing the air out. This type of propulsion is called jet propulsion. In a real rocket, thrust is created by the force of burning rocket fuel as it blasts from the rocket's engine—as the engines blast down, the rocket goes up! Try a different shape balloon and string instead of wire. You can also try tying your wire upward instead of across the room. Write down your results.

air is forced backward

creating a forward-pushing force

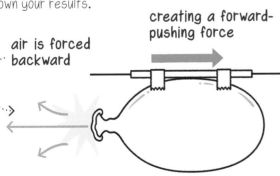

WHO WAS GODDARD?

Robert H. Goddard (1882–1945) was an American inventor who launched the first liquid-fueled rocket in 1926 and came up with the idea of rocket jet propulsion.

Glossary

ACID
A chemical that produces positively charged hydrogen ions when dissolved in water.

AIR PRESSURE
The "push" exerted by air as it presses against something.

ANTHOCYANIN
A chemical pigment (colorant or hue) that makes plants a blue, red, or purple color.

ATMOSPHERE
The layer of gases that surrounds a planet or moon.

ATOM
The smallest part of a substance that can be identified as a chemical element.

AVERAGE
The number that represents the middle value of a range of numbers. To find the average of a group of numbers, add them together and then divide the total by the number of numbers.

BACTERIA
Tiny, single-celled living organisms.

BASE
A chemical that produces positively charged hydrogen ions when dissolved in water.

BIOLOGIST
A person who studies and works in the science of living things (plants and animals).

BOW
To bend under pressure. Also, the front of a ship.

CARBON DIOXIDE
A gas made up of carbon and oxygen.

CELL
The building blocks of which all living things are made.

CENTRIPETAL FORCE
The force that acts on something moving in a circular path to push it toward the center of a circle.

CHARGE (AS IN POSITIVE AND NEGATIVE)
An electric charge that is the property of certain particles, including the electrons and the protons in atoms.

CHEMICAL REACTION
A process by which chemicals combine or change, involving transferring or sharing electrons.

CHEMISTRY
The study of all kinds of chemical matter, including the properties of different chemicals and how they behave and react together.

COMPOUND
A molecule made from two or more elements.

CURRENT (ELECTRIC)
A flow of electricity.

DENSITY
The mass of a substance relative to its volume—it's compactness.

DNA (DEOXYRIBONUCLEIC ACID)
The chemical that makes up chromosomes. It carries information that acts like a recipe for building and maintaining a living thing.

DRAG
The force acting on something moving through a fluid (liquid or gas) that slows it down.

ECOSYSTEM
A community of living things that depend on each other to flourish.

ELECTROMAGNETIC WAVES
Waves that form from charged particles when an electric field comes in contact with a magnetic field. Also known as radiation.

ELECTRON
A tiny part of an atom that carries a small, negative electric charge. Electrons orbit the nucleus of an atom.

ENERGY
The property that makes it possible for objects or substances to do something, such as to move or to make heat.

ENGINE
A powered mechanism used to transform energy and movement from one type or direction to another.

ENVIRONMENT
The surroundings in which an organism lives and that supports a geographically based ecosystem.

EVALUATION
Making an assessment of the value or nature of something.

FIBER OPTIC CABLE
A very thin strand of glass used to carry data coded into pulses of light.

FOUNDATION
Solid base underground in which the walls of a building are rooted, keeping the building stable.